TAKINGCONTROL

LYNSEY DE PAUL AND CLARE McCORMICK

B☘XTREE

DISCLAIMER

This book and the self defence techniques described in it are designed for people of an average level of fitness. Please note, not all defence techniques are suitable for all people. Using the skills demonstrated here without proper care and without practice may result in injury. We recommend that everyone, especially pregnant women, should consult their doctor before attempting any of the techniques demonstrated. In addition, we recommend that you only practise on a cushioned surface and that you wear padded clothes while doing so. In the event that any technique demonstrated causes pain or extreme stress, stop and consult your doctor. The recommendations and advice given to you in this book are not intended as a substitute for expert instruction and medical advice, and the instructions given to you in this book will not provide a guarantee against attack. They are designed to *improve* your chances of survival and escape. The physical self-defence techniques described can be dangerous and are only to be used in the event of an attack against you. They are examples of how to escape from certain sorts of attack. They are not the only ways by which you may defend yourself and/or escape. Real life attacks may differ from textbook situations. It is up to you, the individual, to make your own choices given the circumstances. These choices include whether or not to defend yourself physically.

First published in Great Britain in 1993 by Boxtree Limited

Text © copyright Lynsey de Paul and Clare McCormick

The right of Lynsey de Paul and Clare McCormick to be identified as authors of this work has been asserted by them in accordance with the Copyright, Designs and Patents Act 1988

10 8 6 4 2 1 3 5 7 9

All rights reserved. Except for use in a review, no part of this book may be reproduced, stored in a retrieval system or transmitted in any form or by any means, electronic, mechanical, photocopying, recording or otherwise, without prior permission of Boxtree Limited.

Designed and typeset by Blackjacks, London

Printed and bound in Great Britain by Butler and Tanner Limited, Frome

Boxtree Limited
Broadwall House
21 Broadwall
London SE1 9PL

A CIP catalogue entry for this book is available from the British Library.

ISBN 1 85283 428 5

Front cover photograph by Brian Aris

All photographs within the book © copyright Paul Forrester

CONTENTS

PREFACE

Every woman has the right to be safe. She has the right to go where she wants, when she wants, how she wants – without fear and without danger.

Most men want to protect the women in their lives – their wives, their mothers, their daughters.

This book has been written to help women defend themselves against a violent minority.

In this book we are going to show you how to protect yourself physically and mentally if faced with an attack.

We are going to illustrate basic techniques, such as: frontal attack, attack from behind, on the ground, and hair grabs.

You will learn how every male body has its vulnerable areas and every woman's body has powerful weapons to use against those targets.

AN ASSAULT IS AN ACT OF POWER OVER ANOTHER PERSON

The basic rule of self-defence is to reverse that power, thereby:

TAKING CONTROL

INTRODUCTION

"RAPE MANIAC STALKS LONE WORKING GIRLS"

"KNIFE RAPE HORROR"

"ROADSIDE GANG RAPES BREAKDOWN WOMAN"

It is a sad fact that horror headlines sell newspapers. The ones above appeared in the *Daily Mail* and the *Daily Telegraph*. They have everything: sex, violence and crime. The sort of sensationalism which both fascinates and disgusts the reader.

In the first six months of 1990 there were more than 600 articles on rape in the 10 major national daily newspapers. But at what cost?

A single reported rape victimises thousands of women by making them fearful of going out alone, imprisoning them in their own homes.

One-third of the women interviewed in the 1989 British Crime Survey avoided going out after dark. I found these statistics unacceptable. Instead of being frightened by them, I was outraged.

As little girls we are taught not to talk to strangers, but not what to do if that stranger intends us harm.

There are Rape Crisis Centres, Victim Support Groups and Police Rape Units to help victims after they have suffered an attack, but there is little advice or practical instruction on how women can avoid this kind of danger in the first place or defend themselves if they encounter it. In fact, the police's stance in the eighties was that women should not resist as fighting back might increase their chances of suffering severe injury in an attack.

Women were seen and saw themselves as *victims*, and it seemed to me that this was almost an invitation for a rapist or mugger to attack them, in the belief that he would get away with it.

I found this insulting to women and, as no one else was, felt compelled to do something about it.

I began reading as much literature as I could about sexual violence against women in England and the States: Home Office studies, police reports, crime statistics, studies by sociologists, books by crime defence writers, reports by psychologists. It became evident that the most impressive research into this field had been funded in America by the Justice Department.

The American Justice Department, of which the FBI is a part, carried out a survey over ten years of one and a half million rape cases. The conclusions reached contradicted all previous assumptions. Researchers found that the injuries sustained by women who fought back were no different from those who did not. It was a myth that the risk of injury, be it mutilation or even death was increased by resistance. It was also found that women who used some form of self defence *doubled* their chances of escape.

It seemed everything we had been told before had been *misinformation*. How many lives, I wondered, had been ruined as a result. I felt frustrated and wanted every woman to know what I had found out.

Then, ironically, while I was working on the concept of self-defence for women, I was attacked – by a woman.

I was sitting in my car in London's Trafalgar Square at the traffic lights when a woman wrenched my car door open and began hitting me on the head. I had no idea what had prompted this aggressive behaviour, all I knew was that I was getting hurt. I tried to stop her by putting up my hands but she bent my fingers back. I tried to close the car door but she had wedged herself against it. I thought I had better get out of my car and put one leg out of the car door, forgetting I was still strapped in by the seat belt. I turned to undo the belt and the woman slammed the car door on my leg.

What I did next I have since learnt was entirely wrong. I acted instantaneously out of anger and without considering my actions. I got out of the car to fight this woman. At that time I had not realised that you should only fight if your life depends on it; if there is no other option. I did not stop to think that she may have had a knife or what would be gained by fighting such an irrational person.

Once I was out of my car, I got the worst of it. I had my hair pulled out and my face scratched until it bled. But I managed to land a well-placed kick on her shin which sent her off and got back in my car.

It was 7.30pm on a dark drizzly November night in 1990. I was surrounded by people but no one came to my help. I was extremely shaken and thought, My God, if a woman can do this to me surrounded by people, what could an angry man do to a lone woman in a dark alley?

From that moment I dropped all other work and concentrated only on women's self-defence.

I hired a feature film crew and a commercials director called Kevin Hewitt and funded a frightening six minute film reconstructing three real–life attacks. At the end of the piece I addressed the camera with some hard facts.

I teamed up with the producer Clare McCormick and together we took the project to the BBC who gave us an immediate network slot. We made the BBC 1 documentary 'Eve Strikes Back' which was broadcast in August 1992 and attracted three and a half million viewers – which was three and a half times the expected audience.

I trained for ten months with a 6th Dan black belt ju–jitsu National Coach called John Steadman and discovered that every woman has more potential and more strength than she has probably realised. I am ninety-one pounds (forty-one kilos) and five foot tall, yet I can throw a person off if they are sitting on top of me in a stranglehold. Every woman should be taught such techniques, from school age.

We then made an instructional video on mental and physical self defence entitled *Taking Control*. Boxtree approached us to expand the information given on the video, and so we have written this book.

Self-defence is not just about physical manoeuvres, seventy per cent is mental preparation – the knowledge of how to behave when faced with danger.

Self-defence is not a form of martial arts. I am not suggesting that anyone expects a woman to turn into Bruce Lee or some sort of prize fighter.

Self-defence means taking practical steps to protect yourself, heighten your awareness of danger and in turn build your own self-confidence.

In this book you will learn how to lower the risk of becoming a victim. How to help prevent crime. How to use the natural weapons you have in order to fight and how to target your attacker's vulnerable areas. You will learn how you can buy time to escape, find help and what the best options are if confronted by a criminal.

REMEMBER:

NO WOMAN HAS TO BE A VICTIM

NO WOMAN SHOULD BE TOO AFRAID TO GO OUT AFTER DARK

CHAPTER 1

The Socialisation of Women

The past century has seen unprecedented changes in the lives of women: the right to vote, equal pay, the pill, and the newly recognised status of the female sex as the largest workforce in history.

More recently this pattern of change has continued with the law courts recognising the concept of rape within marriage, and the Synod of the Church of England voting to give women the right to enter the priesthood after two thousand years of exclusion.

But women have had little more than a generation to abandon traditional roles and rules of conduct and morality previously handed down from grandmother to mother to daughter.

In our mother's and grandmother's day, the independent and achieving woman was the exception. There were heiresses, film stars, athletes, and a handful of pioneers like Amelia Erhardt. But they were rare. In the ordinary world, women were employable and marriageable, but only within the boundaries set by men. They had been, as sociologists would say, 'socialised' into certain types of behaviour. They were taught to be submissive, not to raise their voices, not to be rude. They were expected to please, to heal not hurt, to seek approval – in particular men's approval, to be passive. In other words to be:

NICE GIRLS

The Revolution Backfires

The 1960's revolution in attitudes towards sex saw women fighting to achieve equality and respect. The advent of the pill, for instance, brought about a sexual freedom for women never before experienced. But this revolution brought with it a cruel paradox. For some men, with deep-rooted, traditional perceptions of the female role, women could now be divided into Nice Girls who DIDN'T and NOT Nice Girls who DID. The liberated woman was perceived by many not necessarily as a free person worthy of respect but as an easily available sex object.

Media Influence

The portrayal of women as sex objects has been reinforced by the media. In advertising, sex and selling are inseparable from the drink, the aftershave or the cigarette that attracts the beautiful woman, to the car and the chocolate bar which could not be sold without the help of a near-naked nubile.

In the tabloid press, and in pornography, women are displayed for men's pleasure thereby encouraging the perception of them not as equals but as sex objects. This in turn contributes to the undermining of an equal relationship between the sexes.

Fear

In television and film women are for the most part presented as victims, even now. Weak, passive stereotypes who are frequently seen being raped and murdered.

In 1990 the Broadcasting Standards Council conducted a one year study called 'Women Viewing Violence'. It researched women's reactions to violence against women in television and film. The programmes reviewed were a factual programme, a drama, a soap and a feature film all depicting violence and/or rape.

The study's findings were very interesting:

Violence on television did not necessarily increase the level of violence in society, but [that] it did increase the level of *fear*. With regard to violence, the study showed that victims of violence reacted most strongly to violence whereas other groups were affected less. The most striking example of similarity across the groups, regardless of class or ethnicity, was that:

IT WAS NOT NECESSARY TO EXPERIENCE RAPE TO FEAR IT

It revealed a profound anxiety about personal safety, and that, in particular, the film showed that there was a universal identification with the rape victim.

The survey demonstrated that the portrayal of violence towards women, whether fact or fiction, has become the norm rather than the exception in the media.

The stereotypical man when faced with danger is shown as the aggressor, tough physically and mentally. With the odd exception, women facing danger are portrayed as helpless.

All these impressions become embedded in our psyche by constant media repetition – and here we have a dichotomy, a split, a confusion. Are we mere sex objects and victims or are we equals in society? How do women in fact wish to be treated nowadays? How should men behave towards them?

New roles have to be defined, and it takes time for these new roles to make the transition without conflict, to sit comfortably in a changing society.

New Roles for Women

As women, we have taken on traditionally masculine roles in our everyday lives. Many of us are independent achievers and bread-winners, but even with the same backgrounds, education and qualifications, the majority of women still earn less and hold inferior positions to men. By adding masculine characteristics, are we frightened of losing touch with feminine ones?

What should we *learn* and what should we *unlearn*?

Women have to **LEARN:**

- **BEING ASSERTIVE IS NOT THE SAME AS BEING AGGRESSIVE**

- **THE RIGHT TO SAY NO**

- **TO RESPECT THEMSELVES AS EQUALS**

Women have to **UNLEARN:**

- **NOT RAISING THEIR VOICE**

- **BEING EMBARRASSED**

- **NOT BEING RUDE**

- **TRUSTING EVERYONE**

- **BEING NICE**

Repression

Assertiveness is often mistaken for aggression and we are taught that aggression is unfeminine. In our need to gain approval we sometimes suppress our own opinions, no matter who is right or wrong. We collude, however unwillingly or unwittingly, in preserving the common perception of the female role.

This:

AFFECTS OUR SELF-ESTEEM, AND OUR SELF-ESTEEM AFFECTS OUR BEHAVIOUR

Instead of SUPPRESSING our feelings and opinions we have to learn to say 'No!' To contradict without being embarrassed. This is not being rude or unfeminine.

REMEMBER:

YOU HAVE THE RIGHT TO DEFEND YOUR OPINIONS

Once you accept that, you will also accept:

YOU HAVE THE RIGHT TO DEFEND YOUR OWN SPACE

If you are submissive in your everyday life, if you are not naturally assertive, how can you become mentally strong enough to deal with threat or aggression?

These may not be physical. They often start with verbal abuse. At work, some women employees avoid asserting their rights for fear of prejudicing people against them or of losing their jobs. They deny a situation in the hope that it will go away. They want to be NICE GIRLS. This is dangerous. A woman not giving out an active signal of dissent or merely ignoring a situation may result in others assuming that she accepts or even desires it. A woman has to deal with a situation sooner rather than later to make sure that her standpoint is clear. She has to:

GIVE OUT THE RIGHT SIGNALS

Interpretation

Men and women interpret the same behaviour differently. Men are more likely to attribute sexual meanings to what women consider merely friendly behaviour.

In 1985, Bart and O'Brien cited findings from a survey which examined adolescent attitudes towards sex. In the study, half the male students thought it acceptable to have sex by force in certain circumstances. These were:

- **IF THE MAN HAD SPENT MONEY ON THE WOMAN**

- **THE LENGTH OF THEIR RELATIONSHIP**

- **IF THE WOMAN HAD WITHDRAWN HER CONSENT TO SEX AFTER INTIMATE RELATIONS HAD BEEN INITIATED OR HAD 'LED HIM ON'**

Misconceptions

According to Dr Pauline Bart, a sociologist at the University of Illinois and author of *Stopping Rape, Successful Survival Strategies*, a commonly used phrase is that a woman 'turns a man on'. It is as if he has nothing to do with it and the woman is wholly responsible.

This is one of the many myths and misconceptions surrounding the act of rape. Somehow, because it is associated with sex, there is another commonly held misconception: that rape is actually pleasurable. No victim we have met found this to be the case. Instead they experienced years of mistrust, fear and even guilt after such an attack.

Judith Fein, PhD, a self-defence expert in San Francisco, supports Dr Bart's findings that the sexes perceive behaviour differently and explains the facts and fictions of rape.

FICTION: The idea that women want to be raped
FACT: **RAPE IS AN ACT OF VIOLENT AGGRESSION. THE MOTIVATION FOR RAPE IS NOT THE DESIRE FOR SEX BUT FOR POWER**

FICTION: Blame belongs to the woman
FACT: **BLAME AND RESPONSIBILITY BELONG TO THE ASSAILANT *NOT* THE VICTIM**

FICTION: Rape is based on sex and therefore enjoyable
FACT: **RAPE VICTIMS EXPERIENCE INTENSE PSYCHOLOGICAL AND PHYSICAL TRAUMA, SOMETIMES LASTING A LIFE TIME. IT IS VIOLENT AND DEHUMANISING**

IF A WOMAN IS ATTACKED IT IS NOT HER FAULT IT IS THE FAULT OF THE ASSAILANT

Rape and the Law

RAPE IS A CRIMINAL ACT NOT A SEXUAL MISDEMEANOUR

Until recently, certain judges viewed a woman as guilty if she had behaved sexually with the same freedom as a man. Women had to have an almost virginal history in order to be seen as true victims.

However, in 1976 the law changed with The Sexual Offences Amendment Act which disallowed a woman's prior sexual history from being examined in the courtroom, though this could still be allowed at the discretion of the judge.

Jennifer Temkin, Professor of Law at Sussex University and author of *Rape and the Legal Process*, explains:

> In 1976 the law was changed with the Sexual Offences Amendment Act. This stated that sexual history must not be admitted but that defence could apply to the judge who would only allow it if it would be unfair to the defendant to exclude it."

She says that the act has not proven to be too successful. In some cases it was also implied that a woman did not know her own mind. Helena Kennedy, QC, in her book *Eve Was Framed*, quotes Judge Wild's famous directive to a jury in 1982.

> Women who say 'No' do not always mean 'No'. It is not just a question of how she says it, but how she makes it clear. If she doesn't want it she only has to keep her legs shut and she would not get it without force and then there would be the marks of force being used.

This kind of attitude is not only insulting to women but it presumes that rape cannot take place unless there is evidence of brute force. However, many women are intimidated by the threat of violence and submit themselves in order to avoid it. Fortunately, this attitude is not shared by all the judiciary. Ms Kennedy quotes Mr Justice Rougier from March 1990 while sentencing a rapist:

> Women are entitled to dress attractively, even provocatively if you like, be friendly with casual acquaintances and still say 'No' without being brutally assaulted.

Reporting Rape

The figures for reported cases of rape are low. The Home Office and the Metropolitan Police estimate that between 75% and 90% of rapes go *unreported* in the UK. In America and Canada it is estimated that 90% go unreported, while the figure for New Zealand is 80%.

Women fail to report rape for several reasons. Apart from the trauma of court proceedings, there is the fear that the police will not believe them, that they will infer their consent or ascribe blame for provoking the act. Also, statistics show that in over two-thirds of attacks, the assailant is known to the victim and this may pose other dilemmas in reporting the crime.

UK statistics show:

68% of assailants are known to the victim;

32% are attacks by a stranger.

Education

The question arises: how can we prevent these kinds of attack?

Women should take preventive measures to protect their safety and learn basic mental and physical self-defence techniques.

But that puts the onus solely on our female shoulders. The problem should surely be addressed at source. Should it not start with the education of the sexes?

Dr Liz Kelly, Senior Research Officer, Child Abuse Studies Unit at the University of North London, says:

It is fundamental. The process and content of education should be anti–sexist, it should address how children relate to one another, the way that gender is reproduced and how masculinity and femininity are created and constructed.

She says that masculinity is created and constructed against everything female:

'Real' men are encouraged to be the opposite of what women are supposed to be. This is part of the devaluation of women since men are valued more in our society and are accorded more power in every sphere, including the family. What most people want is nice simple solutions. Prevention programmes for children on sexual abuse or bullying make people feel better but have limited effect. Until these issues are integrated to every other facet of their life, their experi-

ences of sexism conflicts with the content of these programmes. What is needed is whole school policies which
challenge traditional roles at every level.

The research undertaken for this book would seem to indicate
that the problem stems from the way both men and women have
historically been educated in and encouraged to play stereotypical
roles within society. New roles must be defined with each sex
taking on some of the other's traditional characteristics.

Dr Jan Stockdale, Senior Lecturer in Social Psychology at the
London School of Economics, says:

> It is helpful to look backward before going forward. Over the
> centuries women have been portrayed in literature, religion,
> popular culture, etc, as representing the highest good and
> basest evil. This has resulted in a number of myths about
> women which have been translated into stereotypes. These
> have been powerful images in gender-role socialisation.
> Society still works hard to try to maintain male/female differ-
> ences. Women – and men – have to recognise that there is a
> wider range of 'acceptable' behaviour for both sexes. Men
> can be permitted closer contact with their feelings and can
> develop qualities of empathy and concern for others,
> together with a reduction of the 'macho' need for dominance
> and aggression. Both men and women have to be encour-
> aged to recognise that it is valid to display behaviours that
> traditionally belong to the other sex.

These roles must be defined by the individual man and woman
and not by traditional codes of behaviour. She continues:

> People have to learn to *take control* of their own 'femaleness'
> and 'maleness' and not let society do it for them.

Conclusion

The conclusion we have reached in this chapter, is that women
must not allow their self-image to be defined for them by society.

SELF-DEFENCE STARTS WITH YOUR OWN ATTITUDE TO YOURSELF AS A WOMAN, YOUR SELF-ESTEEM AND YOUR RIGHTS

In the next chapter you will learn how to lower
the risk of attack by **avoidance techniques** and
by **taking simple precautions.**

PREVENTION IS THE BEST CURE

The basic principle of self-defence is to lower the risks to yourself of becoming a victim; avoid danger as far as is possible. Self-defence means keeping your eyes open and your wits about you.

Statistically, in fact, it is unlikely that you will be attacked. But fear of encountering violent crime is known to be widespread. In a recent TV-am phone-in survey addressing fear which we conducted, 12,161 women called in. Out of that number 10,867, or 89%, said they were afraid to go out after dark. The British Crime Survey concludes that one out of three women avoid going out after dark.

A lot of us fear that we may be mugged or assaulted but:

IT IS FEAR, NOT THE REALITY OF CRIME WHICH MAKES MANY WOMEN VIRTUAL PRISONERS IN THEIR OWN HOME

However, if we take preventive steps to ensure our own safety we can lead our lives the way we wish to. These steps are quite simple and should become second nature.

Travelling Safely
On foot

The lives of all of us are ruled to a greater or lesser extent by the clock, with most of us rushing from one place to another, trying to cut corners. But sometimes those short cuts can be the most dangerous and put us at risk. Perhaps you were late for work and in a rush for the bus stop took that short cut? How many of you reading this have walked down a dark alley because it was the quickest route home? How many of you have cut across parks, heaths, wastelands and deserted areas like railway lines to save five minutes?

According to Sanford Strong, international crime defence instructor and author:

80% – 90% OF ALL SERIOUS RAPES AND MURDERS TAKE PLACE IN DESERTED AND ISOLATED AREAS

Any time you take this kind of risk ask yourself: Is it worth it?

NONE OF THE VICTIMS THOUGHT IT WOULD HAPPEN TO THEM

DON'T LET IT HAPPEN TO YOU

Take the longer route in well–lit areas. Don't let the temptation of the shortest route lead you into danger.

If you are out walking, the police recommend that you walk facing the traffic so that you can see any potential aggressor pull up. Should this happen, yell loudly and run in the opposite direction. If you feel that somebody is following you, cross the road and walk the other way. If he does not continue to follow then you know you are safe. If he continues to follow you then make for populated areas such as shops or houses. Knock on someone's door and ask them to call the police. They do not necessarily have to let you in to do this. If you are near a shop, go in and ask to call the police. Never worry about making a fool of yourself.

REMEMBER:

UNLEARN BEING EMBARRASSED

If you are being followed and you are unable to get to a public area, do not ignore the threat of danger in the hope that it will go away. Turn around, walk in the opposite direction past him and look him directly in the eye, in an assertive, non–friendly manner. This may seem difficult to do but it is important.

DO NOT IGNORE A THREAT

The reasons for this are:

- **You will know if he is NOT a threat**

- **You will know if he IS a threat**

- **Emotionally, mentally and physically you are prepared to deal with an attack. It will be less of a shock and you can be faster in your responses (We will show you how to deal with this in Chapters 4 – 7)**

- **Walk with confidence and purpose**

REMEMBER:

CROOKS ARE LOOKING FOR EASY TARGETS

In America the FBI made a film of ordinary women – mothers and housewives – doing everyday things: picking their children up from school, shopping, or just walking down the street. They showed this film to habitual muggers and rapists in prisons all over America. Each different crook picked out the same women as easy targets from the way they conducted themselves.

You lower the risk of being selected as a victim by being assertive in your manner. Think of yourself in terms of a house. Most burglars do not pick the most difficult house in the street to rob. Crooks are usually opportunist. They avoid the house with alarms, locked windows and doors and choose the house with an open window and less security. Like vulnerable houses, there are vulnerable people.

Keep your handbag close to you. If you are mugged and it is snatched, the police recommend that you do not fight; you should only do so if you are personally threatened. A good tip if you have time is to:

EMPTY THE CONTENTS OF YOUR BAG ON TO THE GROUND

This defocuses the attack from you. Your attacker does not want your handbag, he wants the contents. Another tip is to keep your valuables like purse and keys separately in a concealed pocket or even a plastic shopping bag. Cover up any jewellery.

Hitch hiking

It is *not* recommended that you hitch hike or accept lifts from strangers, no matter how friendly they may appear. This is putting yourself at risk and self-protection is about lowering risks. Remember how in Chapter 1 we saw that men and women interpret the same behaviour in different ways? Not all, but some, men may expect sexual favours in return for your being their passenger.

REMEMBER:

- **WALK IN WELL LIT, PUBLIC AREAS. DO NOT WALK IN ISOLATED AREAS**

- **WALK FACING THE TRAFFIC**

- **WALK WITH CONFIDENCE**

- **KEEP KEYS AND VALUABLES SEPARATE FROM YOUR HANDBAG**

- **DO NOT ACCEPT LIFTS FROM STRANGERS**

There are now some personal safety devices on the market which are approved by the police.

Personal alarms
These are devices small enough to be carried in your handbag or pocket. By pushing a button or nozzle you can trigger a loud alarm which could deter an attacker. Remember that they have to be in your hand ready for use if they are to give any protection. They are available from DIY stores.

Skunk alarm
New on the market from America is the 'skunk' alarm called Repel. This device works like a personal alarm but instead of rendering a noise it gives off a repulsive synthetic skunk-like stench. It is worn on a chain around the neck or clipped to the centre of the bra. A squeeze of the fingers breaks a glass phial, releasing the contents on to the skin. The odour is immediate and is claimed to have a greater impact on a man's sense of smell than a woman's. The anti-dote is a synthetic neutraliser called the Repel Deodoriser which is rubbed on the skin.

Available from Repel Personal Protection Ltd, PO Box 999, Winscombe, Avon, BS25 1AJ.

Anti–rape spray
This is a controversial spray, new on the market, which stains the face of an attacker for up to seven days. It is made from a natural dye and is alleged not to cause pain or lasting damage. From a maximum of seven feet it sprays a thick foam which is intended to obscure the attacker's vision.

It is called Dyewitness.

Travel by Cab or Taxi
Minicabs:
Minicab drivers are not vetted in the same way as Black Cab drivers. There is a higher turnover of drivers and, in general, it is neither possible nor required by law for an employer to vet them. There is no law requiring them to have knowledge of the best

routes or to have anything but a basic driver's licence. It is therefore important to take some precautions when hiring this type of vehicle.

Try and use a known, reputable cab company and, when booking, ask when the cab will arrive and the name of the driver. Do not wait on your own in the street, but get the cab company to telephone you on its arrival. When entering the cab ask the driver his and the company's name to avoid getting into the wrong cab.

A useful tip is to:

WRITE DOWN THE REGISTRATION NUMBER

In the event of you leaving something behind in the car or perhaps suffering some kind of harassment or attack, the driver can then be traced quickly.

Cabs can be expensive but they can be a safer way of travelling alone at night. After public transport stops, they may be the only way to get home safely. If the expense of a cab is a burden for you try sharing a pre-ordered cab with friends. Do not share a cab with someone you do not know.

Outside London, several local councils have now licensed their own minicabs. Some councils will not accept cabs over three years old and they vet the driver's character with the police. These minicabs also display Hackney Carriage Plate numbers on the outside of the vehicle.

Black Cabs:

In general, it is safe to travel by Black Cab. The drivers are given their licence by the Police Public Carriage Office and are thoroughly vetted. They have to pass exams to show a good working knowledge of the roads, which takes two years. Also, a medical check up is required and they have to wear an identifying badge. Nevertheless, take a note of the Hackney Carriage Plate number which is displayed inside and on the back of the cab for reference should you need it.

When driving in London, a cab cannot reasonably refuse to take you less than six miles within the Metropolitan Police Area or one hour's travelling time. This law dates back to the time when carriages were horse-drawn and was passed to spare the horses. Even today all Black Cabs are required by this law to carry a bale of hay, a bag of oats and a bucket of water in their carriage for the horse! Of course none of them do, so technically they are all breaking the law.

Should the driver refuse to take you to your destination within the six mile/one hour limit, you are within your rights to demand that he take you to the nearest police station where you can report him. Failing this, you can report him by giving his Plate number to the Public Carriage Office in Islington.

60% of Black Cabs are owned privately and have one driver, whilst 40% are fleet owned and driven by several drivers. As a precaution, always take a note of the driver's name and appearance.

Travel by Public Transport:

Not only is public transport a quick and easy way to travel, but for many it is the only means of getting around. Although attacks are rare, they are more likely to occur in the late evening. For this reason many women are concerned about travelling alone at night. But there are ways to minimise the risks to yourself.

Buses:

Try and avoid lonely bus stops especially after dark, and sit near the driver on an empty bus. If someone gives you unwanted attention, report it to the driver/conductor immediately.

DO NOT IGNORE A SITUATION WHICH COULD ESCALATE

Alcohol and drunkenness, late at night, are often contributory factors to aggressive behaviour. The offending person can be asked to get off or be dealt with by calling the police.

When there are two or more of you at a lonely bus stop late at night, then stand facing each other, enabling you to see over the other's shoulder for any approaching danger. Remember to be aware at all times. If somebody behaves in a hostile manner or makes you feel threatened, be assertive with them – tell them to stop. If they continue, then walk away from them towards a public area. Remember, never confront unless you have to. Meeting aggression with aggression could escalate the situation. If the bus comes while you are being harassed then report the incident to the driver/conductor. This means you now have a witness who could identify the offender.

Trains:

The same principles apply to travel by train. Try to avoid travelling alone, but if you have to, sit near other people with whom you feel comfortable. If you can, sit near a door for quick exit. If you are on your own and someone gets in whom you feel is a threat, change carriages immediately.

Women travelling in crowded trains may experience covert touching of a sexual nature. If you are molested in this way do not confront the man himself. This makes it your problem and his and separates you from the other passengers. What you need is the attention and support of the other passengers. Recently a woman was indecently assaulted in these circumstances when a man touched her bottom. She took the offender's hand, lifted it in the air, and in a loud voice, said, 'Who does this hand belong to?' The offender got off the train. This kind of reaction defocuses the incident from you and focuses it on him.

REMEMBER:

UNLEARN BEING EMBARRASSED

BE SAFE

Travel by Car

Traffic light crime in towns is on the increase, from simple grabbing of handbags through windows or unlocked doors to incidents, albeit rare, where women have been forced to drive to unknown locations and then assaulted or even murdered.

Whilst in slow or stationary traffic the AA recommend you:

KEEP YOUR DOORS LOCKED

When you stop in traffic, leave enough space between yourself and the car in front so that you can see its back tyres on the road. This means that you have enough space to manoeuvre your car should there be any trouble. Should a stranger try to enter your car or break a window you will be able either to drive away out of the gap, or else to drive forwards and backwards, making entry very difficult.

In the unlikely event that you look like being the victim of a serious assault where a stranger enters your car and tries to force you to drive somewhere else, there is some advice we can offer.

Our natural instincts when threatened can be summed up in the phrase 'fight or flight'. But when a dangerous person intimidates a woman, her natural responses may be overwhelmed by fear. She is too scared. In this situation, as in any assault, you have to chose the best of the bad options open to you.

REMEMBER:

NO CROOK WANTS A WITNESS

This type of man is basically a coward and a bully. He is not a terrorist, he is not willing to die for his cause. He wants an easy target.

MAKE IT AS DIFFICULT FOR HIM AS YOU CAN

Sound the horn, yell, drive into a stationary object, jump out.

WHATEVER YOU DO:

DO NOT ALLOW HIM TO TAKE YOU TO ANOTHER LOCATION

Break this rule and the risk to you *doubles*. Crime scene number one is where you encounter a criminal. Crime scene number two is where he may take you. If he could commit the crime where he meets you, he would do so. Crime scene two is going to be better for him and worse for you or he would not take you there. Your best chance for escape is sooner rather than later. Respond quickly.

Parking
Wherever possible:

REVERSE INTO A PARKING PLACE

This gives better control and an easier exit. Lock all doors and windows and keep all your valuables out of sight. Always have your keys ready when returning to your car.

Even if you leave your car for only two minutes, *lock it*. There have been incidents reported where an assailant has concealed himself in the back of a car. Always check your car when you return.

If you are parking a car in the day and will be returning to it after dark, assess what the locality will be like at night. Is it a well-lit, busy and safe area? Remember, things look different at night.

In multistory car parks, park as near to the attendant's office as you can and make a note of where your car is parked.

Long journeys / motorway driving

Let someone know where you are going and your estimated time of arrival. If there is no one to tell, then write it in your diary or leave a note in your home. This means you can be traced if anything happens.

Keep your car serviced. Before setting out, check your petrol, tyres (carry a good spare tyre), water levels, and oil. Carry a road atlas, a torch, petrol can, walking shoes and extra coat in case of breakdown. The AA says that the majority of breakdowns are caused by flat batteries.

Breakdowns

In the event of a breakdown, pull over to the hard shoulder as far off the motorway as you can. Switch on the hazard warning lights. Exit the car through the *passenger's* side. Do not get out of the driver's side as your car door may extend on to the motorway and cause you and others serious injury. Leave animals in the car with a window slightly open for air.

Walk in the direction of the oncoming traffic following the arrows on the small 100 yard marker posts to the nearest SOS telephone. You do not have to be a member of a motoring organisation to use the SOS phones. Emergency calls from the orange SOS phones are free. There is no dialling tone so do not assume that the phone is not working.

You will automatically be connected to a police control room. Give the police your vehicle make and model, colour and registration, and the nature of the breakdown. If you are a member of a motoring organisation, give them your membership number. If you are not, and you do not have money with you, tell the police. They will not abandon a car on the hard shoulder and will deal with it. If you are alone, inform them. Ask for the name of the breakdown service to expect and ask the service for identification when they arrive.

In the event that the SOS telephone is out of order, then walk back past your car and to the nearest phone the other way, so that you are never too far from your car.

Once the emergency call has been completed, return to your car, walking as close to the green verge as you can, and wait on the embankment so that you can see the recovery vehicle arriving. The AA states that one in eight motorway deaths occur on the hard shoulder. The risk of being hit by another car is far greater than the risk of personal attack. If you choose to sit in your car, then sit in the front passenger seat and fasten the seat belt. You are further away from the oncoming traffic and it gives the impression that you are not alone.

DO NOT:

- **CROSS THE CARRIAGEWAY**

- **ATTEMPT REPAIRS TO THE OFFSIDE (NEAREST THE MOTORWAY) OF THE VEHICLE, EVEN CHANGING A WHEEL**

- **USE THE HARD SHOULDER EXCEPT IN AN EMERGENCY**

Should someone stop, get back into your car and lock the door. If they offer help, explain that the police have been informed. Trust your instincts. If you are in any way suspicious, then write down their vehicle make, model, colour and registration number. This may deter anyone with the wrong intentions and could be helpful to the police.

If you are disabled, carry a large sign asking passing motorists to 'CALL POLICE'. Put this in the side window nearest to the motorway as routine police patrols may take time to pass by. Check you have this sign with you before you set off on your journey.

Motorway organisations membership telephone numbers
AA: 0256 24872 Call out: 0800 88 77 66
The AA now has an emergency-only telephone called 'AA Callsafe'. It works like a car phone and plugs into the car cigarette lighter. Calls can be made only to the AA by dialling 111 and to the emergency services by dialling 999. The phone can be transferred from one car to another and is ideal for women, disabled people and motorway drivers. 'AA Callsafe' is available at main AA shops, through some newspaper direct mailing and from the Automobile Association, Freepost (BZ 47), Basingstoke, Hampshire, RG21 2BR.

RAC: 0800 550 550 Call out: 0800 82 82 82

National Breakdown: 0532 393 666 Call out: 0800 800 6888
The National Breakdown service has a 'Lone Woman Scheme'. This costs £20 per tow away for non–members. Membership costs £57 per year for nationwide assistance which includes all costs.

Preventive Measures

Burglary is on the increase but:

80% OF ALL HOUSE BURGLARIES ARE NOT PLANNED

In three burglaries out of ten, entry is gained through an open door or window. If your house looks secure, you are less likely to be a victim of this sort of crime.

REMEMBER:

CROOKS WANT EASY TARGETS
CROOKS DO NOT WANT WITNESSES

If they have to break glass or force a door it means they might be seen or heard. Your home is where you should feel safest and although a break-in may not be life-threatening, it is a violent intrusion and can be most traumatic. Apart from the loss of valuables, your home may be vandalised.

Help safeguard your personal effects by using marking kits which are available from DIY shops. Etching with an etching tool, engraving or even invisible ultra-violet markers will identify your property if recovered. Your initials and address would be sufficient.

Burglar alarms

These range from expensive units professionally fitted to simple DIY kits. You can get free advice from your local police and quotes from burglar alarm or insurance companies. If you arrive home and suspect that there is an intruder, do not enter the premises.

REMEMBER:

NEVER CONFRONT UNLESS YOU HAVE TO

Go to a neighbour or phone box and call the police. If you enter the house and disturb a burglar, get out as fast as possible. Do not block his exit or confront him in any way. Thieves can panic and unintentionally cause you injury. Do not touch anything.

If you are awakened by an intruder at night, again, do not attempt to confront him. If you can get out of the house safely, then do so. If you can, lock your bedroom door and call the police. If you are alone, pretend to call out to someone else.

If you are physically attacked alone inside your home it is equivalent to being attacked in an isolated area. Create as much noise as you can to alert your neighbours or a passerby. This might mean your breaking a window to get attention. (We will deal with physical attacks in chapters 4 – 7)

Locks

A thief does not like locked doors or windows. If a door is locked he has to enter and exit through a window. If the window is locked then he has to climb over broken glass. The more precautions you take, the more it will deter him.

MAKE ENTRY AS DIFFICULT AS YOU CAN

Contact reputable lock manufacturers for free estimates or call your local Crime Prevention Officer at your nearest police station for information and guidance.

For front and back doors, mortise dead locks and strong security chains or door limiters are advisable. Sliding bolts also add to your security. It is best to fit locks on every window.

Spyholes

Fitting a spyhole means you can identify a caller without having to open the door. Always ask for ID cards from gas, electricity and telephone workmen and even the police. Do not let strangers into your home unless by prior appointment.

REMEMBER:

UNLEARN TRUSTING EVERYONE

80% of burglaries occur when premises are unoccupied. This can mean whilst you are out for a few hours or for extended periods like holidays. Remember to cancel milk and newspapers and tell your neighbours to alert the police should they be suspicious. Your neighbours could also help by making sure your mail is not conspicuous by collecting it or pushing it through the letter box.

Lighting

Time switches for your lights are available at DIY stores. External lighting, in particular sonar lighting which works when somebody approaches the area, is a useful deterrent to any potential thief.

In the next chapter we will deal with **mental self-defence** – how to prepare yourself mentally if faced with a threat or physical danger.

CHAPTER 3

AN ASSAULT IS AN ACT OF POWER OVER ANOTHER PERSON

The basic rule of self-defence is to reverse that power, thereby:

TAKING CONTROL

Self defence is not just a matter of physical manoeuvring; 70% of it is mental preparation, the knowledge of how to behave when faced with danger. Without this mental discipline, you cannot successfully put into practice the physical aspects of self-defence.

The first principle of self-defence for women is to disable your assailant long enough for you to escape and find help. This is called:

BUYING TIME

In this chapter we will consider your options if you are faced with an attack or the threat of one, as well as the misinformation and myths on the subject of violent attacks which women have been conditioned into accepting.

Misinformation

The first piece of misinformation commonly promoted is that if you resist an assault, you will escalate the injuries you suffer and increase the chances of mutilation or death. Extensive studies in America now show that this is not the case and that the level of violence in any attack is determined not by the victim, but by the assailant.

America has funded more research into the epidemic of violence than anywhere else in the world. The Justice Department, of which the FBI is a part, studied over one and a half million cases of rape during ten years of research. Findings showed conclusively that injuries sustained by women who fought back were the same as those who did not. Where victims were seriously injured, it made no difference whether they resisted or not.

FBI statistics from 1991 concluded that women were three times as likely to escape attack when using some form of self-defence.

Another myth is that woman may excite an attacker by fighting back. Dr. Pauline Bart, the celebrated sociologist at the University of Illinois and author of *Stopping Rape: Successful Survival Strategies*, refutes this:

...In no instance in my research did the assailant say when a woman wasn't resisting... this is very boring. I am going to have to find a black belt in karate to get turned on.

Neither does fighting an assailant make him angry; you must accept that this kind of criminal is *already* angry and looking for someone to vent this anger on. An assailant acts as he does because of a need to assert power over someone else, from a desire for domination and violation, not sex.

Avoidance strategies

The Queen's Bench Study, 1976, showed that women who avoided rape used more defensive techniques than women who were raped. American research shows that talking by itself, simply pleading or being passive, were all behaviours exhibited by rape victims. Indeed, they may even lead to a victim being raped.

Attackers are not looking for equal partners to fight when they pick women.

ATTACKERS ARE LOOKING FOR EASY TARGETS

An assailant expects you to be submissive and to play the role of victim. By doing so, you are giving him exactly what he wants. You have to break that script. Don't play his game. Make it as difficult as you can for him. If you have the option to flee, then take it. Never confront or fight unless you have to.

FIGHTING IS THE LAST OPTION, THE LAST RESORT

NEVER CONFRONT UNLESS YOUR LIFE DEPENDS ON IT

Strategies which have been found to work are a combination of:

- **YELLING, MAKING NOISE, ATTRACTING ATTENTION.**

- **FLEEING OR TRYING TO FLEE**

- **ENVIRONMENTAL INTERVENTION**

- **PHYSICAL RESISTANCE**

Make as much noise as you can. Yell, so that everybody can hear you. Remember: no attacker wants a witness. Yelling from the diaphragm gives you a shot of adrenalin and helps you breathe, whereas screaming can constrict your throat. If you have an opportunity to escape, then take it. The environment is also a factor. If there is a passerby you can call to, or a shop you can run into, or a house where you can knock on the door, *then do it*. And, lastly, if there is no other option but to fight, then be prepared to fight. (We will deal with physical defence techniques in Chapters 4-7)

Instincts

Women are by nature instinctive. Our instincts are our *first* warning system, but few adults have trained themselves to listen and respond to their instincts. Most adults try to analyse, second guess, wait and see. It is better to respond immediately.

TRUST YOUR INSTINCTS

During the course of our research, we discovered from hundreds of letters sent in by women who had suffered attack that they had felt a *sense of threat* before the incident.

One woman, jogging by a canal, saw a man tying his shoelaces in front of her. Her first instinct was to turn around and run the other way. Intellectually there was no obvious threat, but instinctively she felt danger. Her NICE GIRL conditioning did not want to offend this stranger and so she ran on past him and was attacked. She put herself at risk rather than listen to her instincts.

ACT ON YOUR INSTINCTS

THEY ARE YOUR FIRST WARNING SYSTEM

Control

The longer you leave him in control, the worse it becomes for you as a victim. Crime escalates with time. Take a hypothetical scenario of a burglar entering a house with the sole intention of stealing. He finds a woman on her own and sees the added opportunity for rape. This completed, he panics and the crime escalates to murder.

TIME WORKS AGAINST THE VICTIM

CRIME ESCALATES WITH TIME

Confronted with crime, you have to act quickly; in reality it happens extremely fast.

You may hear of people who successfully talked their way out of an attack, but the odds of achieving this are against you. Certainly if you are not immediately attacked, then you may have time to be aggressive and use verbal skills to escape. But the truth is you do not often have time to analyse a criminal.

DO NOT ANALYSE AN ATTACKER

What you are trying to do in effect is be a street-corner psychoanalyst in a crime that takes only seconds. Most attackers are experienced, are very likely repeat offenders and are prepared. Trained analysts who treat them for months in hospitals and prisons get it wrong. They may release these offenders back into society and:

70% OF OFFENDERS REPEAT THEIR CRIMES

A criminal will say and do anything to get control over you. He will promise you anything, he will threaten you with everything.

IT IS THE NATURE OF CRIMINALS TO LIE

NEVER BELIEVE THEM

Our natural instinct is 'fight or flight', but when we are intimidated that instinct may be overridden. A woman, when threatened with physical violence and ordered to obey, may think that by obeying she will not be hurt. It seems likes a fair deal. But a deal only works if the person you are dealing with has your value system, if he has some code of honour.

MAKING DEALS WITH CROOKS IS MAKING DEALS WITH LIARS

Criminals are not like you. They do not have your value system. An angry, irrational criminal does not know himself what he is likely to do and to rely on his word or to put your safety in his hands is a big mistake.

EXPECT NO MERCY FROM AN ATTACKER

If you are threatened with a weapon but an assailant does not show it, there is a 50/50 chance that he does not have one. Remember that a criminal will say and do anything to get control. If you have a chance for escape, then take it sooner rather than later. Run! You are better off running from a man with a knife than standing two feet from him.

IGNORE THREATS OF VIOLENCE
FOCUS ONLY ON WHAT YOU MUST DO TO ESCAPE

Anger

When a rapist attacks a woman the first thing she is likely to feel is fear. She may even freeze with fear and be unable to move or scream. This is exactly what he wants. He is relying on the woman being too weak to fight back. He does not want or expect her to be angry enough to defend herself.

The most important emotion to get in touch with, therefore, is your *anger*.

TURN YOUR FEAR INTO ANGER

Studies carried out by Dr Pauline Bart showed that women who were most likely to avoid rape were not only angry but enraged at their attacker for daring to intrude on their space. She says:

> ...the angry women recognised danger early, at the first unwanted approach. This early recognition helped them avoid rape. Women in self defence classes learn the necessity of constant awareness and the early recognition of danger... The women who were more likely to be raped did not realise they were in danger until they were attacked.

Self esteem plays a large part in a woman's anger. Judith Fein, author of *Are You A Target?*, says:

> A woman who knows her own feelings and who respects her own integrity also knows that it is right to become angry and outraged and does not let the anger turn inward... she directs this anger combined with the readiness to support it physically, if necessary, at the rapist.

If you are physically attacked, you have to behave in a way you probably never have before:

YOU HAVE TO BECOME UNCIVILISED

If you are attacked and there is no option other than to fight, you have to *fight with everything you have from the outset*. You cannot wait to assess how bad the attack is going to be. If someone grabs you physically then on a scale of one to ten – you have to fight at level ten every time. You have to use surprise and speed as a weapon. You have to turn the situation around and make it *yours*. You have to:

TAKE CONTROL

If you are attacked, or you feel you may be attacked, these are the *key points* to remember:

- **TRUST YOUR INSTINCTS**

- **RESPOND QUICKLY**

- **GET ANGRY**

- **ACT UNCIVILISED**

- **YELL! MAKE AS MUCH NOISE AS POSSIBLE**

- **FOCUS ONLY ON WHAT YOU MUST DO TO ESCAPE**

- **FLEE IF YOU CAN**

- **BE PREPARED TO USE PHYSICAL FORCE**

- **EXPECT NO MERCY FROM AN ATTACKER**

Sanford Strong interviewed over two hundred people who had been victims of crime for his forthcoming book *Strong on Defence*. Apart from rape victims, interviewees included men, women and whole groups who had been viciously assaulted. Further evidence was gathered from a criminal prosecutor and the police and some of the victims of crime he had known over his twenty years of service with the San Diego police force.

He found that there were five characteristics shared by people who survived or escaped attack:

1. ALL HAD DRAWN THE LINE

They had all considered what they would and would not do if they were faced with attack. They had made decisions ahead of time, they were **mentally prepared.**

2. THEY EXPECTED TO GET HURT

It may come as a shock to you, but in reality you have to accept that when facing a violent crime, you will probably be hurt. You must also accept that you can only choose from the options open to you and that they are 'lousy' options. You have to choose the best of the lousy options. These survivors accepted that they would suffer injury in order to escape and survive.

3. THEY REACTED QUICKLY

It is important to act quickly. Your best chances are sooner rather than later. No one waited for a better time or the 'right' time. They realised it may not come.

4. THEY FOCUSED ON ESCAPE

They ignored the threats made against them and concentrated on one thing only – trying to escape. They did not focus on their injuries or the crime being committed against them.

5. THEY WOULD NOT ALLOW THEMSELVES TO BE CONTROLLED

They had an overwhelming fear of being controlled and sub-jected to the savagery of a criminal.

To conclude this chapter we repeat the golden rule that should never be broken. It is of vital importance and cannot be stressed enough:

NEVER BE TAKEN FROM CRIME SCENE NUMBER ONE TO CRIME SCENE NUMBER TWO

Crime scene number one is where you confront a criminal. Crime scene number two is where he may take you.

If crime scene number one was a suitable place to commit the crime, he would commit it there. If an assailant has to take you somewhere else in order to commit the crime, *do not go*.

Crime scene number two will be worse for you and better for him. It will be isolated, you will not be able to choose it, and in the event of injury you will not be able to get help. He will have complete control.

80% – 90% OF SERIOUS RAPES AND MURDERS HAPPEN IN ISOLATED AREAS

The disappearance of estate agent Suzy Lamplugh and murders of Julie Dart and fifteen-year-old school girl Helen Gorrie took place in crime scene number two. Estate agent Stephanie Slater, who survived her kidnapping and assault, was locked in a box in crime scene number two. She escaped because she was released, not because she got away. She was lucky.

As Chapter 2 showed, the vast majority of serious rapes and murders take place in isolated areas. Crime scene number two will almost certainly be such a place.

Jean O'Neil of the National Crime Prevention Commission of America is categorical in her opinion that you should never allow yourself to be taken to a second crime scene. She says:

The FBI's Violent Crime Research is adamant that one of the times you do whatever you have to do to escape, is when a criminal tries to take you to another location.

REMEMBER:

NEVER ALLOW YOURSELF TO BE TAKEN TO ANOTHER LOCATION

FOCUS ONLY ON ESCAPE

TURN THE SITUATION AROUND AND TAKE CONTROL

In the following chapter we will deal with a woman's natural weapons and a man's natural targets.

EVERY MALE HUMAN BODY HAS ITS VULNERABLE AREAS

EVERY WOMAN'S BODY HAS POWERFUL WEAPONS TO USE AGAINST THOSE TARGETS

We have all heard about different ways of defending ourselves within the law. personal alarms, keys between your fingers. Just remember, anything you carry must be in your hand ready if it is to be of any use.

However, you have **five natural weapons** which you carry with you at all times.

- **YOUR HEAD**

- **TWO ARMS**

- **TWO LEGS**

If someone attacks you:

NEVER ADDRESS WHERE HE ATTACKS YOU

For example, if his hands are around your throat do not attempt to force his hands off your throat. That would be might against might and he is stronger than you. The art of self defence is strategy against might, speed against might and surprise against might.

REMEMBER:

S S S

STRATEGY

SPEED

SURPRISE

GO STRAIGHT FOR THE VULNERABLE AREAS

THE VULNERABLE AREAS ARE:

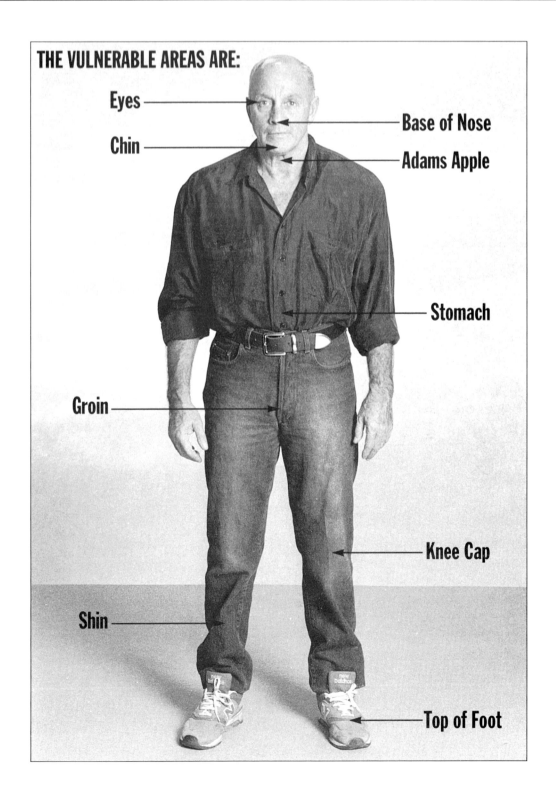

Eyes

Chin

Base of Nose

Adams Apple

Stomach

Groin

Knee Cap

Shin

Top of Foot

Natural Weapons

Fig. 1 CLAWING

Clawing is very natural to a woman. The principle is to claw straight into the face of an assailant, damaging the eyes and raking the face with as much force as you can.

Fig. 2 PALM HEEL OF HAND

Bend your fingers and hand back, tensing your hand as hard as you can to make a strong weapon. Use the base of the palm above the wrist. You must keep it tensed at all times to avoid injury to you.

Fig. 1 CLAWING

Fig. 2 PALM HEEL OF HAND

Palm Heel

Fig. 3 TOP FIST

Fig. 4 BOTTOM FIST

Fig. 3   TOP FIST

Clench your fist hard, wrapping your thumb tightly around and *out-side* your fingers. Again, always keep your hand tensed for maximum power.

Fig. 4   BOTTOM FIST

This is the same principle of tensing and wrapping your thumb around your fingers but using the bottom of your hand to strike.

Fig. 5   BACK FIST

a) Again the same clenching and tensing of the hand but using the back of your hand.
b) Be sure to keep your wrist, hand and arm in a straight line. Tense the arm as well as the hand as strongly as you can. Hit in one sweep and follow through, as if you were playing tennis.

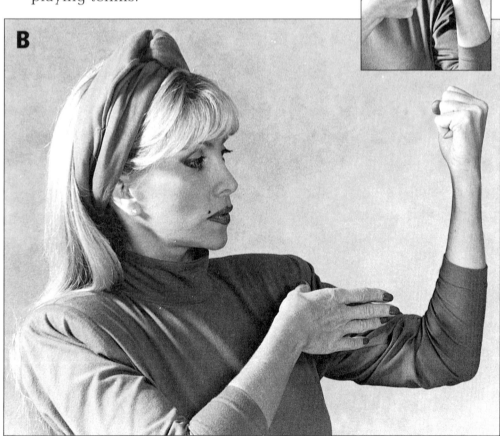

Fig. 5 BACK FIST

Fig. 6 ELBOW

Fig. 6   ELBOW
Draw your elbow back fast in a straight line, like you are opening a drawer. Keep your upper and lower arm tensed and clench and tense your fist.

Fig. 7   STAMPING
Stamp as hard as you can on the *top* of your assailant's foot. Use the heel of your foot for maximum injury. Think of stamping through the foot to the ground.

Fig. 7 STAMPING

Fig. 8 KICKING

Fig. 8 KICKING

a) When you kick, stand at an angle to your assailant, keeping your knees slightly bent. This aids your balance, keeps your centre of gravity and helps you kick. It is not possible to kick effectively with straight legs. Turn your body from the hips to face him.

b) Keeping your balance and your centre of gravity, bring your knee up. Try to keep your body upright, do not lean forward. This prepares you for the kick.

c) When you kick, snap the bottom half of your leg out at the target and bring it back quickly again to make sure you retain your balance. This kind of kick is called a 'snap–kick' because you literally snap your leg out and snap it back again.

Natural Targets

IT TAKES ONLY 8½ POUNDS OF PRESSURE TO BREAK MOST BONES IN THE BODY

When practising these moves, remember to do them slowly and gently. These moves are effective and **will** cause injury if practised at full speed and force. Full speed and force should only ever be used in the event of a real attack and *at no other time*.

Fig. 1   EYES
One of the most vulnerable areas of an attacker is his eyes. Claw straight into the face as hard as you can.

Fig. 2   NOSE
Use the palm heel of your hand and push up under the nose where the base of the nose meets the face above the lip. Hit hard and follow the movement through.

Fig. 3   CHIN
Again, use the palm heel of your hand, keeping it tensed, and hit up and underneath the chin. This forces the head backwards and will cause him to lose balance.

Fig. 1 EYES

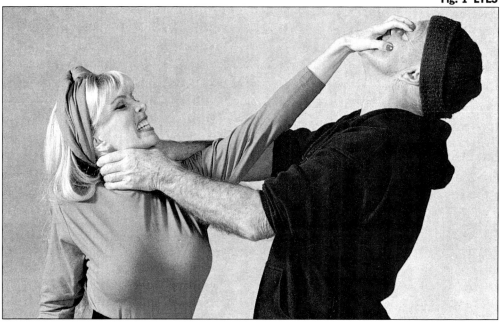

Fig. 2 NOSE

Fig. 3 CHIN

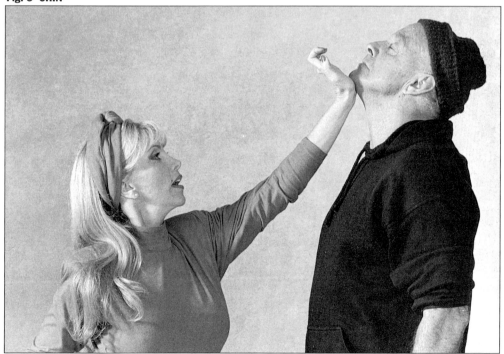

Fig. 4 CLENCHED FIST TO GROIN

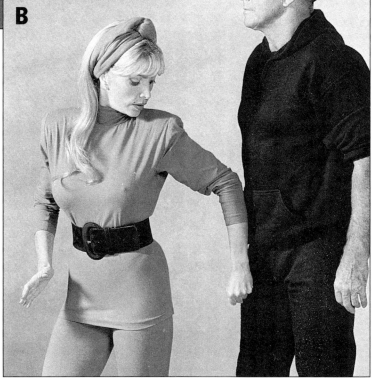

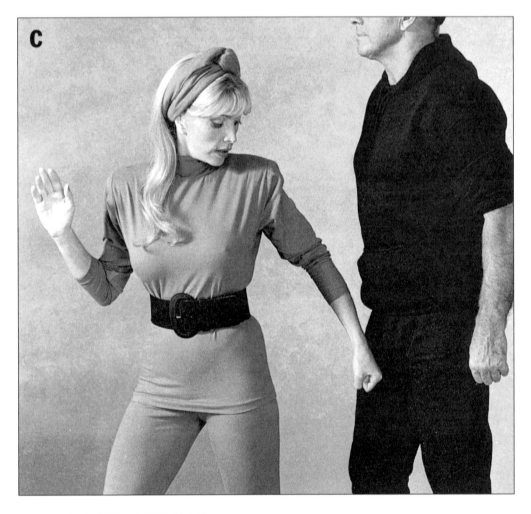

Fig. 4   CLENCHED FIST TO GROIN

a) Top fist:
    Hit to the groin area with your top fist. Use all the weight of your body to follow through to maximise the impact. This would be used in a frontal attack.

b) Bottom fist:
    Hit to the groin area with your bottom fist again using as much body weight as you can. This would be used in an attack from behind.

c) Back fist:
    Alternatively, you can use the back fist in an attack from behind. Whatever is more convenient. Remember always to tense your arm and hands.

In the next chapter we will deal with **frontal attacks** and **attacks from behind**.

**C
H
A
P
T
E
R
5**

The first principle of self defence is to disable your assailant long enough for you to get away. This is a vital means of buying time, escaping and finding help.

As we said in Chapter 4, you have **five things** to fight with:

- **YOUR HEAD**

- **TWO ARMS**

- **TWO LEGS**

Fig. 1

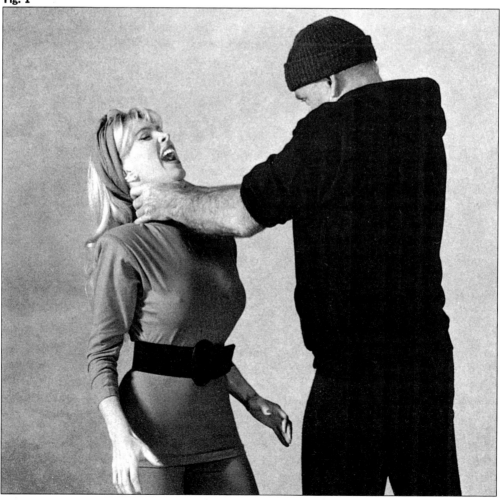

If someone grabs you or your clothing HE **has effectively tied up**
TWO **of his five defences.**
You have all FIVE **left.**

GO FOR THE VULNERABLE AREAS

Attack from the Front
Front stranglehold position

Fig. 1
In this front stranglehold the assailant has grabbed the throat,
thereby tying up two of his defences and leaving his vulnerable targets open.

Fig. 2
Reach up IN BETWEEN the assailants arms, CLAWING INTO THE FACE.

    Do not try to claw by reaching around the outside of his arm as
he may be able to block you before you can do any facial damage.

Fig. 2

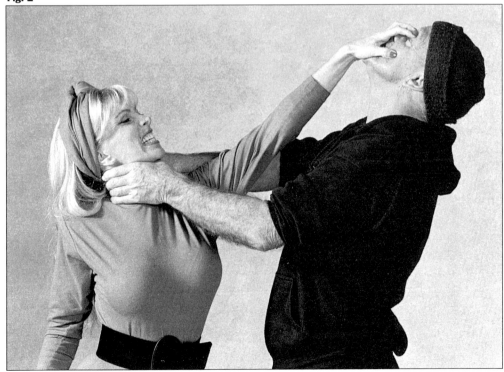

Fig. 3

Fig. 4

Fig. 3
Still clawing to the assailant's face and eyes, push his face as hard as you can. This will make him lean backwards, so making the groin area more accessible.

Fig. 4
Still clawing to the face and eyes, hit with your top fist to the groin as hard as you possibly can.

Fig. 5

If you have time to kick to the groin then do so. Hit as many targets as you can to disable him before running to find help.

Fig. 5

Once you have disabled an attacker RUN. The principle is:

HIT AND RUN

REMEMBER:

ON A LEVEL OF ONE TO TEN, ALWAYS FIGHT AT NUMBER TEN.

You must never hold back as you do not know how bad the attack or the force used against you might become.

Attack from Behind
Back choke

Fig. 1
This is the most common form of attack on women. In this back attack the assailant has grabbed the neck in the crook of his arm and has the other arm around the body.

Fig. 2
The principle is to hit as many targets as you can but do not worry if you miss one. First, stamp on the top of his foot with your heel.

Fig. 1

Fig. 2

Fig. 3

Fig. 3
Following that, 'head butt' back into his face with the back of your head. Bring your head back sharply to make contact. If he is taller than you then drop down a little and come up under his chin.

Fig. 4
While he is standing directly behind you, his vulnerable groin area is not accessible. Your own body is blocking the target. Push your hips out as far as you can to the side. Making a space like this enables you to hit or grab the groin. Hit with your bottom fist or grab the groin, twist and pull out.

Fig. 4

CHAPTER 6

Hair Grabs
Ends of hair

Fig. 1
In this hair grab, the assailant has hold of the ends of the hair, pulling the head backwards.

    The natural response for most women is to pull away:

DO NOT PULL AWAY
THIS WILL HURT YOU AND NOT HELP YOU

Fig. 1

Fig. 2

Turn around quickly to face your assailant. He will not expect this and you will be taking him by surprise.

REMEMBER:

S S S

Claw into his face and eyes, pushing as hard as you can.

Fig. 2

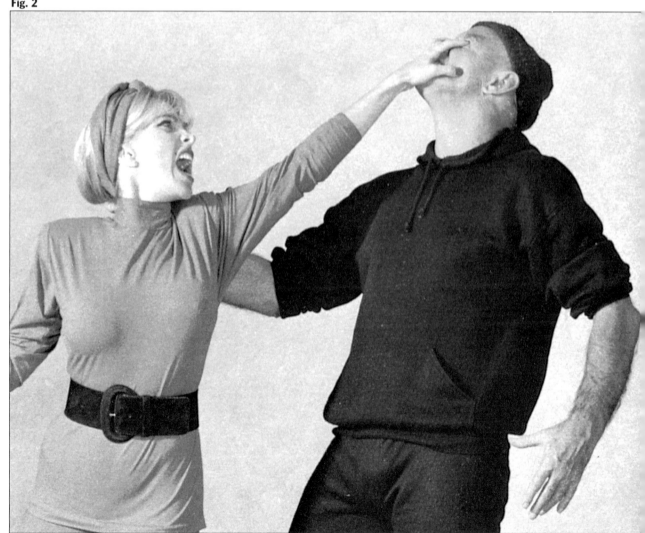

Fig. 3

Clawing and pushing hard to the face will cause him to lean away, thereby making his vulnerable areas accessible.

Fig. 3

Fig. 4

Hit hard to the groin with your top first, still clawing to the face. If you have time to kick the groin or any other target then do so.

Fig. 4

Top of hair/head

Fig. 1

In this hair grip the assailant has hold of the top of the head by grabbing your hair.

Fig. 2

SOMETIMES IT IS TO YOUR ADVANTAGE TO HOLD ON TO THE ASSAILANT

Trap his hand and fingers onto your head by pushing his hand down hard on to your head using BOTH your hands.

Fig. 1

Fig. 2

Fig. 3

Fig. 3 a), b), c)
Drop down slightly and still pushing down hard trapping his hand, TWIST SHARPLY to face him. DO NOT LET GO.

Your body is stronger than any man's wrist and this action will put a 'wrist lock' on him, causing extreme pain. Dropping down will give you more control. The lower you are, the more pressure you put on his wrist.

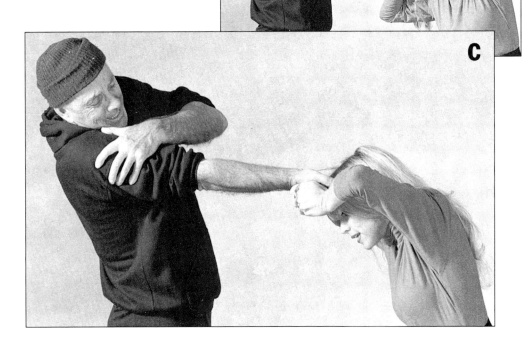

Fig. 4

Still grasping his hand to your head, kick to the groin.

    Whenever you hit or kick, repeat the action until the assailant is disabled and you can run away.

REMEMBER:

PRACTISE THESE MOVES SLOWLY AND GENTLY

These techniques can be dangerous and are only to be used at full force and speed in self-defence against an attack.

Fig. 4

**C
H
A
P
T
E
R

7**

Ground Attacks
Rape position

Fig. 1
In this ground attack, the assailant is in a rape position, lying between the legs. The principle of the defence here is to throw him off you as soon as possible and then to disable him by targeting his vulnerable areas.

Fig. 2
Grab his ear or his hair and with the palm heel of your hand push up hard underneath the nose.

Fig. 3
In self defence:

WHERE THE HEAD GOES – THE BODY GOES

Pulling his ear (or hair) and pushing up hard under the nose with the palm heel of your other hand, twist and push his head to the side. Roll with your body in the same direction.

Fig. 1

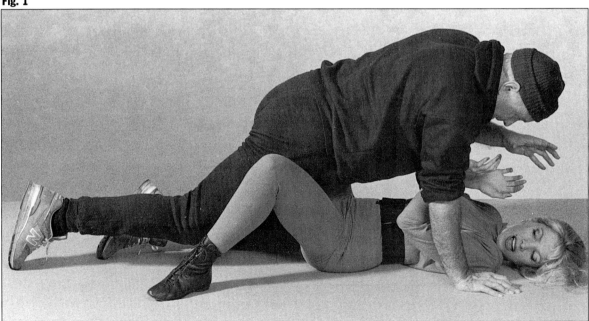

Fig. 2

Fig. 3

Fig. 4

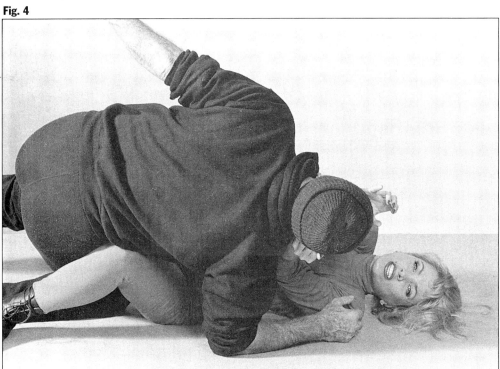

Fig. 5

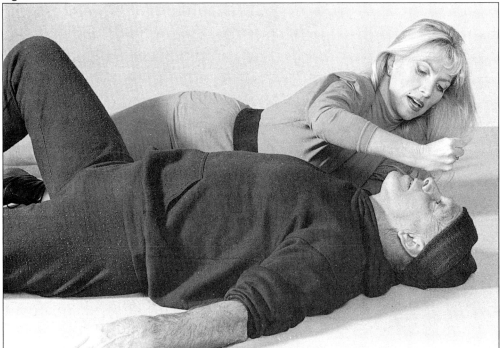

Fig. 4
Keep hold of his ear and nose until he is off you.

Fig. 5
Hit to the nose with your bottom fist.

Fig. 6
Hit to the groin with your bottom fist.

WHENEVER YOU FIGHT, GIVE IT EVERYTHING YOU'VE GOT

You do not know how bad an attack may become.

REMEMBER:

EXPECT NO MERCY FROM AN ATTACKER

Fig. 6

Shoulder pin

Fig. 1
As with all the ground attacks, the object of your defence is to throw your assailant off you and then to disable him.

In this 'shoulder pin' the assailant is sitting on top of the body, pinning the shoulders down with his knees.

Fig. 2   a), b), c)
Arch your body up as high as you can. This will tip him forward, causing him to lose his balance.

At the same time, continuing to arch your body, bring your knee up and knee him sharply and forcefully in the back. Knee him more than once if you have to. This will cause him to fall forwards.

Fig.1

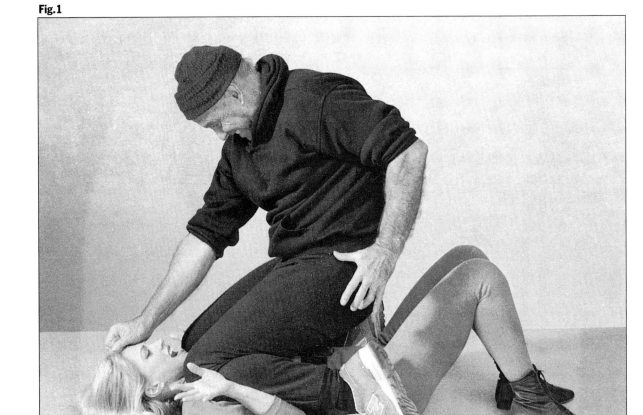

Fig. 2

Fig.3

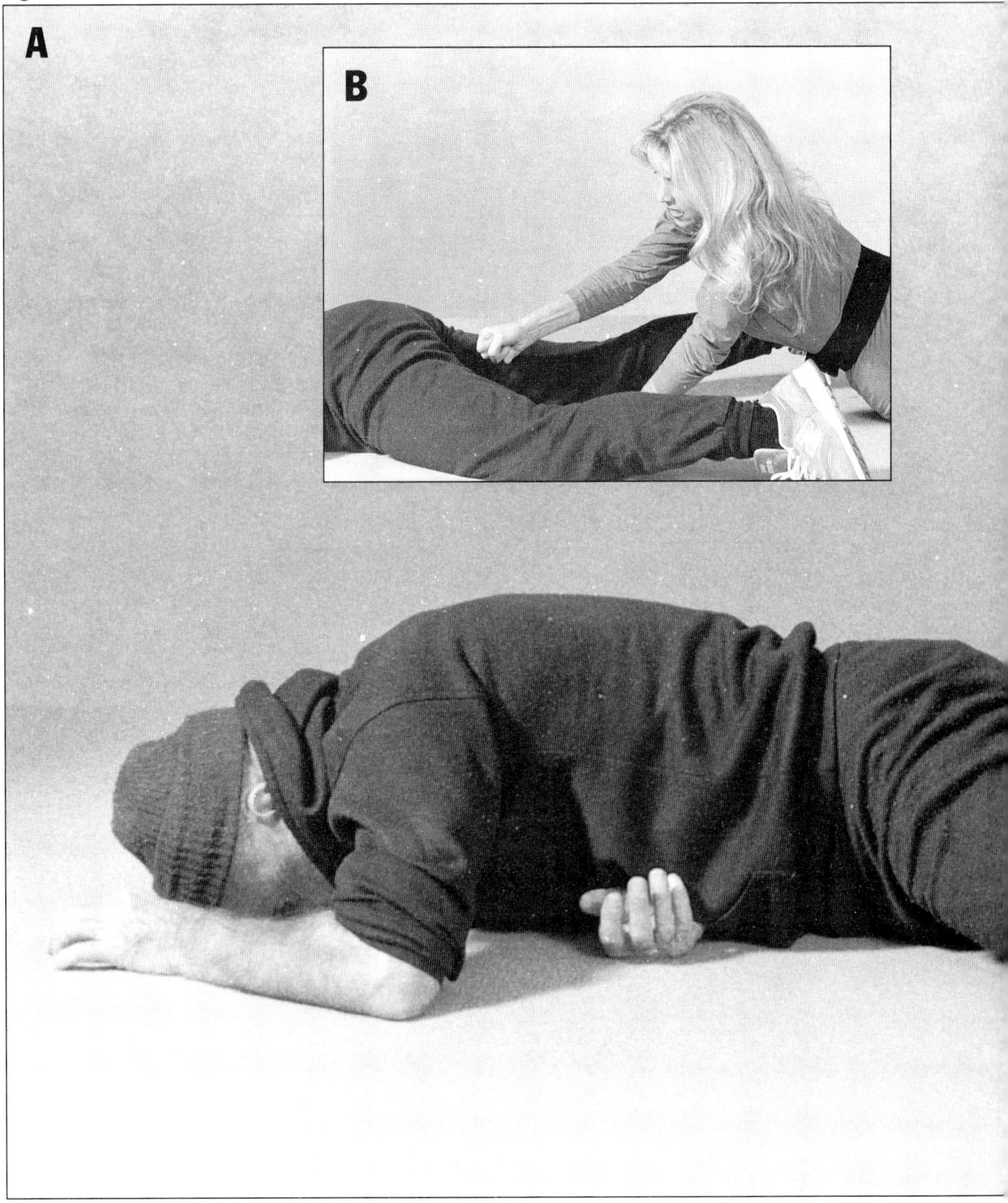

A

B

Fig. 3   a), b)
Hit between the assailant's legs to the groin with a clenched fist.

Ground front stranglehold

Fig. 1
In this ground attack the assailant is sitting astride the body with both hands around the throat.

REMEMBER:

IN ANY STRANGLEHOLD HE HAS TIED UP TWO OF HIS DEFENCES

YOU HAVE FIVE LEFT

Fig. 1

Fig.2

The first principle of self-defence when trapped on the ground is to throw the assailant off you as soon as possible.

To do this you are going to have to use your hips, legs and arms.

Fig. 2
In preparation for throwing him off, draw your knees up into a bent position, spread your legs either side of his legs.

Fig. 3   a), b), c), d)

Weave your arm over one of his arms and under his other arm, placing your hand behind his elbow. Hit your hand behind his elbow with your other hand and push him to the side using both your hands. His elbow is vulnerable when pushed in this way. What you are doing is forcing it against the way it works naturally, in the opposite direction.

REMEMBER:

IT TAKES ONLY 8½ POUNDS OF PRESSURE TO BREAK MOST BONES IN THE BODY

Fig.3

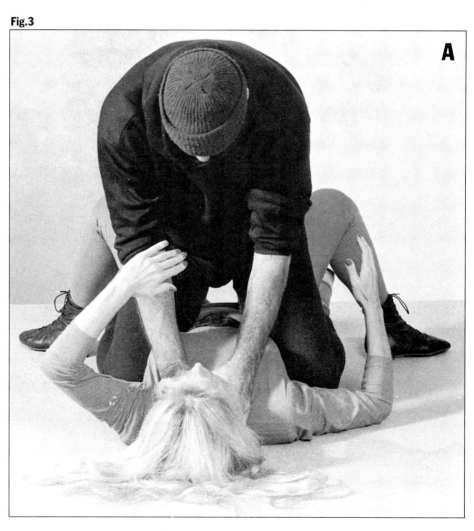

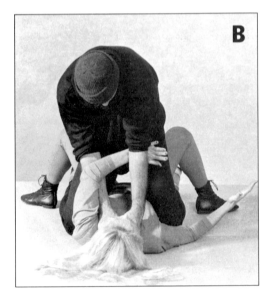

Fig.4

Fig. 4   a), b), c)
At the same time, use your hips and legs to twist and push him off. It is important that you roll with him, trapping his leg underneath you.

Fig. 5
Thrust your top leg/knee into his groin at the same time targeting other vulnerable areas like the face/nose.

Fig. 6
If you are able, hit to the groin with the bottom fist.

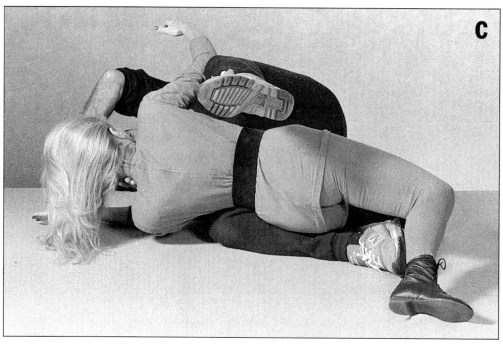

Fig.5

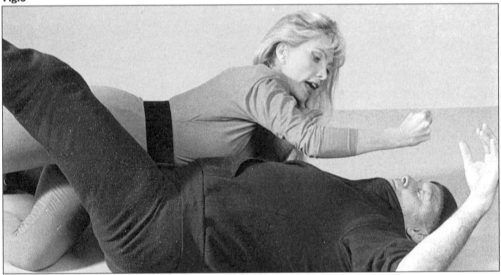

Fig.6

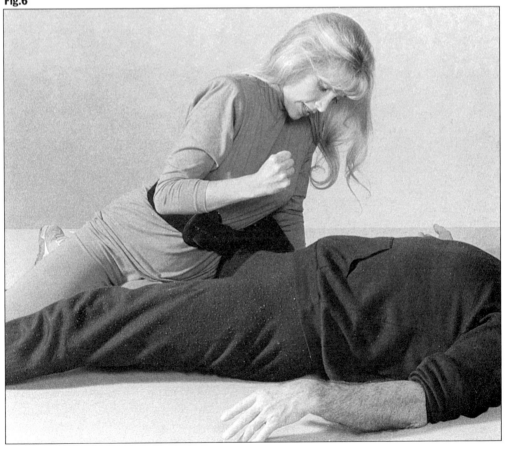

CHAPTER 8

The following are true stories, the personal stories as told to me in interviews of women who suffered attacks ranging from indecent assault while travelling on the bus to rape with violence.

In my introduction I talked of the sensational horror headlines in the press which sell newspapers and are all we ever read about. Seldom do we read about the women who got away – about the success stories.

Here are twelve.

1 Caroline: Indecent Assault

Caroline is an attractive, voluble twenty eight year old who lives with her boyfriend, Christopher. Three years ago, after working on an exhibition stand in The Ideal Home Exhibition in London's Earls Court, she was travelling home on the tube at around quarter past eight in the evening when she was attacked by a young man.

I had been working on a stand in the Ideal Home Exhibition at Earls Court. I had one glass of champagne, nothing more, and around eight o'clock took the District Line home on the tube. I got on to the train at the last carriage because when I get back to my station, it's easier for me to get up the steps and straight on to the high road, so it's not lonely. I sat near the doors next to the glass partitions because there's the emergency button to hand if anything should happen. Living in London, I always take precautions because there are so many strange people around,

especially at that time of night. Everybody's gone home for dinner and there aren't that many people on the tube.

I was sitting there with about ten other people and we set off. When we got to Hammersmith, everybody got off and left me alone with this young boy. He was about nineteen years old, had blond curly hair, was clean-shaven and nicely dressed with a pair of jeans and a bomber jacket. He actually looked like somebody's brother. He was a little taller than me and I'm five foot eight and a half so he was probably five nine, five ten. He was slim and looked like a teenager, nothing sort of threatening except he made me feel uncomfortable. He didn't stop looking at me. I was doing normal things like reading the paper, but it was when he came and sat next to me that my heart started to flutter a little bit.

He asked, 'Could you tell me how to get to Acton Central?' which is another major line station. I said to him, 'Oh, you're on the wrong train, I'm afraid,' and he said, 'Right, OK,' and put his hand on my knee.

Now I was wearing a smart business suit with a skirt just above my knee, not very short or anything. I brushed his hand away and stood up. He said really aggressively, 'Sit down, where do you think you're going?' And he started to breathe quickly in an excited way. I sat down again,thinking, we're in between tube stops. I wanted to try and keep things calm and normal so I started chatting away. I just kept talking. My major concern was not to alarm him until we got to a stop. I tried to stay cool, but inside I was quaking and my heart was beating. I think I would have felt even more nervous but for the glass of champagne I had had earlier.

We got to the next stop, not my station, and I got up to get off. I thought I'd get up quickly and get out but he managed to get to the doors before me. He grabbed me by the shoulders and banged me against the glass partition. I said, 'I'm not going anywhere, just thought I'd stand up, you know.

Then the train set off again and by this time I was feeling very intimidated. All I could think of was that I had somehow to push the emergency button, that I had to get help because along that track it's very dark and there aren't a lot of people about at that time, so even if I'd got off the train, what would I have done? I'd have been alone on a dark station.

I reached for the emergency button, but again, he got there first. He grabbed hold of me and started pushing me around and slamming me against both partitions. He was really throwing me around. I didn't do anything. All I was trying to do was get my mind around the problem.

Then he let go of me and went to the top end of the train. It was really weird because it was as if I were behind the glass partition looking at the situation, like looking down on it, like I was a spectator. He came back towards me completely exposing himself – everything was hanging out, and at that particular moment I thought; Caroline, you're either going to get knifed or raped here, what do you do?

So I looked at him and thought; My God, who does he look like? And I thought he looked like my little brother as I had one of a similar age. So as he was coming towards me I took a deep breath and said in a strong voice, 'Sit down and put that away!' And he did. He sat down and said, 'Don't talk to me like that.' And I said, 'Oh I'm terribly sorry, I always talk to people like that. I'm bossy.' And in an attempt to take control of the situation I said, 'Now, you want to get to Acton Central, let's talk about it.'

God knows where I got the strength from really. I was shaking, I was a nervous wreck. I think I aged about ten years. I just kept talking, I didn't want to give him a chance to intimidate me further. I talk a lot as it is, but I think I really outdid myself that night.

He then began threatening me verbally, saying things like, 'Don't you talk to me like that or I'll do things.' He was shaking and breathing heavily and was still exposing himself. He was also furious, absolutely furious.

I felt I had to make it a familiar situation in order to handle it. He was sitting where the two double seats face each other and I was still standing by the glass partition. I wasn't leaving that door for anyone. There he sat, threatening me, and I said very assertively, 'Now come on, let's change the subject. You want to get to Acton Central. Have you got any money? You have to change stations...' And I was talking and talking and talking and talking and talking until we got to the next stop when he came up towards me again. I banged open the door and grabbed hold of his arm and pushed him out of the train with me. He ran one way and I ran the other.

I ran to the ticket collector and said, 'I've just been attacked.' And the ticket collector said, 'What do you expect me to do about it?' So I said, 'Well, I think you'd better get the manager.' So the manager came out and I was taken to his office and the police were called.

The police didn't think that it warranted actually coming out to speak to me, they just spoke to me over the telephone. At this particular moment my feelings were confused. I began to think perhaps it was me, perhaps I caused all of this wearing a shortish skirt, you know – all silly things. I was saying things like, 'He was only young, he was only about eighteen.' You know, really stupid, stupid things. Making excuses for him when it was his fault.

When I finally got home, Christopher, my other half, wasn't in that evening so I called a friend who shot round. As soon as he got there, I just burst into tears. I was in a terrible state for weeks after that.

A week later a policewoman came around to see if I was all right and to take yet another statement. But let's face it, a week later is a bit too late, isn't it? I asked her what I should do, how could I travel alone without feeling scared? And she told me to take an umbrella with me even if it was hot because I could be done for assault if I carried an actual weapon. But I couldn't travel on the tube alone for two years, I was so upset. It's only recently that I am able to get on the tube by myself. If I went out, Christopher would have to collect me, even if I worked late, and I mean we're talking seven o'clock.

That man made me feel very vulnerable, but I think as women we are capable of using our brains and actually intimidating some of these men. He was trying to dominate me, so I just switched it around, I reversed it. I took control.

You discovered that this man had actually attacked other women didn't you?

Yes. Several weeks later, I was watching Crimewatch on television and they put up an identikit picture of a man who had attacked two other women in the Holland Park area, on the tubes. I said to Christopher, 'My God, that's him!' And I telephoned the police and told them I knew who it was. They suggested that I do what is called a 'surveillance', which would have meant travelling on the same train again with two plain clothes policemen to see if I could spot my attacker. Luckily he was caught so I didn't have to do that. I never heard from the police after that.

Would you say to other women that it is good to be assertive in such a situation?

Yes, I would. It doesn't help if you sit there looking extremely vulnerable and hiding behind a big coat or a magazine. If you are in that situation it is probably better to act as if you are in control and not intimidated by people looking at you, that it doesn't bother you. I think these men like to dominate and you must not let them.

Looking back, do you think you could have done anything else to help yourself?

Maybe I should have changed carriages when the other people got off, but you don't think it's ever going to happen to you. You're sitting there going home from a day working where you've met lots of strangers and you just don't think it's going to happen to you. And then it does.

2 Lesley: Attempted Rape with Violence

Lesley is 22 years old and from Norfolk. She works as an assistant manageress in a wine bar in Covent Garden. She was attacked in Smithfield Meat Market whilst out with friends for the evening.

It was July last year and I'd been out with friends for the evening when we landed up at Smithfield Market at a cafe in the early hours of the morning. I needed to go to the toilet, but there wasn't one in the cafe. The owner told me there was a public toilet just outside.

I couldn't find the toilet anywhere, so I walked down an alley and got to the bend in it when this guy appeared around the corner. It was four o'clock in the morning and still very dark and it was very quiet, there were a few guys around in the meat market.

I didn't feel nervous to begin with, but I instantly felt that I shouldn't have been where I was. I didn't look at him because I didn't want to invite anything, or by the fact that with me looking at him I thought he would sense I was nervous. So I just kept on walking until he walked past me, then I turned around and followed him out of the alleyway because I knew if I broke into a run I wasn't going to make it back to where my friends were if he attacked me.

We got to nearly the end of the alleyway and he turned round and came towards me. I thought, Oh, he's forgotten something, he lives up there, or he's going back for something. And then I thought. He's going to grab me. And I thought, No, don't be so silly. All of a sudden he grabbed me around the neck with his arms and tried to pull me to the floor.

I didn't do anything, I couldn't, I was sort of pushing him away but I wasn't screaming because it seemed too unreal. Then as he pushed me to the floor I realised what was going on, and let out a huge scream and he put his hand over my mouth. He was behind me and his arm was around me and I was in a ball, so I couldn't kick out and started wriggling. His hand was over my mouth and I couldn't breathe and I totally panicked. I thought, This is it, I'm going to die. I couldn't see any way out of the situation that I was in. I kept thinking that my friends would realise that I'd been away for a long time. It seemed like twenty minutes but in fact when I got back they said I'd been away for less than five minutes. Then I thought, If they did come looking for me they wouldn't know where to find me. I thought about being found dead in the alleyway and I also thought about my mother.

I kept thinking that somebody would come and save me, but there was nobody else around. It was four o'clock in the morning and I realised nobody was going to get me out of this. I had to find some way to get out of it myself or I was going to die, so whatever I did didn't matter because I didn't have anything to lose.

So then I just went for it. I wriggled, pulled, got his hand away from my mouth so I could breathe and bit his forearm very hard. I bit so hard that I thought that a chunk of his arm would come off in my mouth.

I did think as I was biting him that he could become violent and maybe smash my face in but it didn't seem to matter. He loosened his grip and I jumped straight up and ran. When he had pulled me to the floor I was facing out towards the exit of the alleyway and as I got up, I ran the wrong way back into the alleyway, into a courtyard, a dead end.

So just as I thought that I'd got away from him I experienced the fear that he might be walking back up towards me, he might be waiting for me at the bottom of the alley, so I screamed and screamed. I let out four or five long screams because I didn't know what to shout. I was really scared and didn't know if anyone was around. I started banging on windows. Nobody came out, nobody put on a light, nothing. So I thought, Maybe these are offices and there's no one around. And knew that I was far better off being close to the end of the alleyway so I ran for it.

I ran back to the cafe, screaming and crying for my friends to get the police. My friends kept saying, What's happened? What's the matter? It seemed too much to explain to them what had actually happened. They went to call the police and then shortly after that the police drew up outside. Somebody had heard my screams in the alley and had called them. I had blood all over my T-shirt but I felt really dirty that I'd had his arm inside my mouth.

The police put me in the car and drove me to the end of the alleyway and said, Is this where it happened?

They looked around and then took me to a police house. They were really good to me and had a doctor there. I didn't want to be examined, because I thought I was fine. They took a swab from the inside of my mouth and blood samples too. I had bruises and scrapes from the cobbles. I also had a bump on my head. They took my statement but I couldn't tell them what he looked like. He was taller than me. I am five foot one inch tall. The policeman said, Did you hear him coming? I said, No. So, to explain, I said, He was wearing trainers and in my mind he's quite a scruffy sort of guy.

The police put me in touch with victim support because I didn't feel comfortable anywhere and I felt extremely vulnerable. It was also this realisation that every man if they wanted to could do that to me and every man had physical strength over me.

Victim support were really good and said, It's perfectly OK, it's all right, you're not making a huge great thing out of nothing. Because I felt that I was, in a way, guilty. A few people have said to me, What on earth were you doing down an alleyway at that time of night? And when you look at it like that, yes, it was pretty stupid, but that doesn't mean that I was asking to be attacked or that I would automatically have been attacked by going down there. I should have just as much right to go down an alleyway, if I want to, and not have my space invaded. So that feeling turned to anger as well, but at the time I felt a bit silly.

Victim support also said that when you have an experience like this, it's like you've bereaved yourself. It is as if part of you has been taken away and it makes you re–value things and look at things differently as well. I was alive and that was the most important thing.

What would you say to anyone reading this book, what advice would you give?

What I would say to other readers is that I felt that I had nothing to lose by fighting back and if anybody else is in a similar situation, don't let the bastard get one over you, don't let them win. Fight back.

3 Betty: Mugging

Betty, whose husband was in the diplomatic service, is a lively youthful sixty year old who was attacked ten years ago whilst walking home from a late work shift at Reuters, where she was P.A. to the security advisor. It was eleven o'clock on a dark November night when two young men ran up behind her and one tried to steal her handbag. In the case of Betty the two men really picked the wrong woman. Her petite feminine looks and her age belied the fact that she was a black belt in karate.

It was ten years ago when I was on shift work, and I'd come home from a late shift at the office. I took the train to New Southgate railway station which is very deserted at that time. The station is next to the mental hospital and there is a long lonely approach from the station to the main road.

I was alert as usual but what I didn't do that day was put my bag across my shoulder the way I usually do, because I think I was feeling a little sleepy. I had a carrier bag in one hand and my handbag looped up around my other hand. I started to cross the road and I didn't know it at the time, but two young men who had just come out of the drinking club saw me as I walked along the road.

I must have been holding my handbag quite tightly because I felt the tug on it. I thought: Oh – he's trying to take my handbag. I turned around and suddenly there was this mass of wet tweed in my face. I was face to face with a mugger.

He was about twenty-three years old, short and quite heavy and slightly taller than me. Believe it or not it is easier to handle a tall thin man than a short stocky one because the centre of gravity of a small man is nearer the ground. I dropped my carrier bag but kept hold of my handbag, grabbed his jacket lapels and we started sort of waltzing around the pavement.

I said, 'You're not going to have it. If you want to play rough, I'll play rough.'

He kneed me in the groin. That hurt a bit but it's not the same for a woman as it is for a man. Little did he know but I had trained in karate for many years and was a black belt, and although it had been ten years since I trained it is something you never forget. I let out a loud yell from the diaphragm that I had learnt called 'Kai'. The reason for this yell is that at the point of contact this shout, this explosion of air, tightens the body and prepares you for fighting. This came quite instinctively; however, I was also trying to intimidate him a bit. I wasn't angry, I thought, This is fun.

I didn't say anything and everything seemed suspended in time. I just went through the motions. I did a hip flip, which is a very basic move in karate and very easy for a woman to learn. It doesn't require a great deal of strength, it doesn't require a lot of lifting power, it is just from the lower hip. I twisted him over and we ended up in the gutter with me sitting on top of his chest.

I was pinning his wrists to the ground when his accomplice came up behind me and asked, 'Lady, lady, are you hurt?' I said, 'No, call the police!' He said, 'Please, let him go.'

I looked over my shoulder and he disappeared down the road. He'd panicked when he saw what was happening. I was trying to flag down buses and cars but nobody stopped. They probably knew that the mental hospital was just across the road and I suppose they thought that two patients had suddenly escaped at eleven o'clock at night and had decided to do something in the gutter. Every time I tried to flag down cars, the young man would grab hold of my scarf and try to pull it. I would then have to hit him in the face with a clenched fist and pin him down again. This happened over and over again. It was almost too ridiculous for words! I was getting a bit angry because nobody would stop.

A bus pulled up and I said to myself, 'Oh at last!' But the driver just looked out of his door and then moved off. I thought surely he was going to stop but he didn't. A couple came along and asked if they could be of any help.

I said, 'Yes, please, this man tried to snatch my handbag, would you please call the police?' They went away and in no time at all, the police arrived.

By then quite a crowd had gathered around us and the man was standing on his feet, some-what dazed. The police took one look at his face and thought *he* was the mugging victim. Later on I saw a picture of his face, and it really was a mess. I didn't know at the time, but he was well known to the police as a petty criminal with convictions for cheque book theft, breaking store windows and crimes of that nature. The funniest thing was that he was making all sorts of excuses for his sorry state like, 'The pavement was narrow', or 'She shoved me!' The pavement at that point was six feet wide.

He finally admitted that he had tried to mug me and went to court. He got six months.

Were you badly hurt?

I got hurt a bit. I scraped the top of my foot, my instep and my knee. I was a little bit sore. The police advised me to see the police surgeon for a general check up which I did in case the evidence was needed in court. I didn't have to go to court because he admitted the crime.

The police always recommend that people should only fight back if their personal safety is at risk and for no other reason. Did you think about that?

No, I just thought, He's not going to get away with it. There are so many vulnerable people in this world and if you take one villain out for just a while it's better than nothing!

So what would you say to women reading this book who may find themselves in the same position – of being attacked in this way?

I would say don't lie down and take it. I would also say that you have to be prepared for such an occasion. Have in mind a set of rules that you lay down beforehand, and practise them. When I walk along the street now I look at men and size them up. I try to find their vulnerable points.

Do you recommend that women should take training?

I think they should because it would give them a certain amount of self-confidence. I think that you really need to go to professional people. Women are very strong but they don't like to realise how strong they are sometimes. They think it's unfeminine to be strong but I don't think so. I think it's very important and it is also good for your well being, you feel better.

There are two types of training. You can train as a sport or take it more seriously like I did with my Japanese Sensai (instructor) called Suzuki. I also recommend that women should work with men as much as possible because a man's weight and strength is different. You don't realise until you work with men how important that difference is. You don't understand the force you would have to use until then.

If you hadn't taken training do you think it might have worked out differently?

It might well have. He might have got the bag away, I don't know. But it was very funny. When the police arrived, my handbag was still on my elbow.

He picked the wrong woman didn't he?

Yeah, he did pick the wrong woman. On the other hand he might have picked the *right* woman because I'm glad to have had the experience!

4 Joyce: Attempted Rape

Joyce is thirty-five years old and works as an accounts clerk in Cumbria. The attack on her happened on a wintry February night as she was walking back from her friend's house.

It was eight o'clock on a cold wet February evening, so as you can imagine I was all wrapped up with boots, trousers, the lot. I was walking back home after visiting a friend when I noticed a man coming round the corner further up. I had an eerie feeling and sensed that something wasn't quite right, but shrugged it off.

We passed each other and then the next thing I heard were footsteps running up behind me. I had a feeling that he was coming for me but I thought: No, it can't be happening, it's not happening.

You think it's never going to happen to you, especially in a small town like Barrow-in-Furness where everybody more or less knows everybody else and you think you're quite safe, but you're not safe anywhere.

The footsteps got louder and closer and the next thing he grabbed me from behind. He was tall, about five foot eleven, stocky with dark hair and a big moustache. He was what I would call a slob. Not a nice person at all. He put both hands around me with one hand over

my mouth and the other holding both my arms down. Now normally when my husband grabs me playfully, because I'm just under five foot, I can always slip under his grip, but I couldn't get out of this man's grip and I was also in shock. I couldn't yell either as his hand was over my mouth. I remember smelling drink on him so I knew he was probably drunk.

He started to march me towards an alley, he couldn't rape me where we were as there were people walking around on the street. He told me he had a knife. I was terrified when all of a sudden he let go of the arm that was over my mouth and then I started pleading with him.

I said, 'Let me go, just let me go.' He said, 'No, shut up. Don't look at my face.' I kept pleading and said, 'I've got two children at home. I won't tell anybody, just let me go.' 'No, shut up. Don't look at my face.'

As we got into the alleyway he pushed me against a wall. I suppose anybody passing by would have thought we were just lovers, having a bit of a mess about. He unbuttoned my coat and put his hands inside my jumper and opened my bra and fondled my breasts. He was kissing my face and my neck. He kept saying to me, 'Kiss me.' I just kept my lips tightly shut. There was no way I was going to return a kiss I just stood still.

I thought, Well you can do whatever you like, but you're not going to get any comeback from me. I'm not going to return anything to you.

And because there were people passing by he couldn't go any further. Because he had said he had a knife, what kept going through my mind was self- preservation. I kept telling myself to keep calm and that my chance would come and when it came I would take it. With me being so small and with him being at least a foot taller than me and very stocky, I thought, You'll not easily fight your way out of this one. But something inside of me just kept saying, You're going to get your chance, there's no way he's going to rape you, you'll get away. But I did fear for my life. I kept thinking of the two sons I had at home and how much they needed me. I thought that if I called out for help and he stabbed me, that would be the end of me. He could lash out and get me in the throat. I didn't want to take that chance. I'm the type of person who keeps calm in a crisis. I break up afterwards.

He'd obviously decided we were going somewhere else and he got hold of both my hands so that I couldn't run off, one arm around me holding my left hand and the other hand of his in front holding my right hand and we walked along the alleyway.

An old man walked past and I thought of calling out to him, knowing that as long as his hands were on mine, he couldn't reach for his knife. But the man was old and I knew that my attacker could easily flatten him and that I could make the situation worse by making him any more angry.

Further along the road I saw a younger man and at that moment his hand loosened its grip as we stepped down off the pavement. I saw my chance.

I pulled my hands away and ran across the road to this man and said, 'Help me, help me, you've got to help me, he's going to rape me.'

My attacker came over as bold as brass and said, 'Keep out of it, it's a domestic dispute.'

I couldn't believe it. I said, 'Jesus Christ. I don't know him.' Luckily this guy believed me and he stood his ground and kept me away from my attacker, and with that my attacker took a swing at him and, as he ducked, I ran into a pub across the road, screaming like an idiot. They must have thought I was loopy.

I just went in and said, 'Phone the police, phone the police! There's a man out there who just tried to rape me, you've got to phone the police!   And they just stood staring. It seemed like ages before anybody did anything and called the police.

I remember somebody said to me, 'Give her a drink, give her a stiff drink.' What flashed through my mind was, If they smell drink on my breath, they're going to think I'm drunk and lying and they might just let it all go.

The police came and they said, 'Will you come in the car and see if you can find him?' So they put me in the car and we drove to the next street. My 'knight in shining armour' was holding my attacker down on the ground. I said, 'That's him. Be careful, he's got a knife.' I never even told my rescuer that he had a knife, I should have done. I never actually saw his knife, I don't know if he actually had one.

I spent two hours in the police station telling them my story. I had to strip in front of a policewoman because they had to take my clothes away for forensic evidence, in case he denied it. She had to check me to see if I had any scratches or bruises as well.

When I got home I got into the hottest bath I could stand because I felt so dirty.

The man was taken to court and he pleaded guilty, luckily, so I didn't have to go. And he was sent away for psychiatric reports and that was the last I heard. When I went back to the station for my clothes, the CID said to me that he'd come out of jail in September the previous year. He'd been in jail for raping two women. The officer said he'd go away for a long time where there was no drink and no women and would have to be a good boy – and then they'd let him out. I think probably the next time he could kill somebody, and there's not a thing you can do about it.

What would you tell women who find themselves in the same position?

Well, you've got to keep calm, because if you go crazy you're not in control. You've got to read the situation and pick your moment. It could be that if you swing round you could catch him off guard straight away. Knowing what I know now having done self-defence, I would have reacted differently.

Tell us about your self-defence and what you learned in your first lesson?

I took up Aikido. Aikido isn't lashing out, it isn't hurting anybody, it's basically getting away from an attacker. Having said that, my instructor did show us a couple of things that could knock somebody out if the need ever arose. I learned how to fall in the first lesson without hurting myself. I felt so exhilarated and believe that everybody

should learn first aid and everybody should learn to protect
themselves. There are more
attackers out there now than I
think there ever were.

I shall never forget my attack
and I will never forget how to
get away from an attacker. It
may get rusty over the years and
I may need to refresh my style,
but I won't ever forget how to
get away now. It's deeply
embedded in my subconscious.

5 Patti: Armed Robbery

Patti is a vivacious and glamorous actress in her early thirties, born in Nigeria. She lives with her husband Stephen and two children in a detached house on a busy road in Surrey.

Six years ago, she was alone in her house with her fifteen-year-old niece, her six-year-old daughter and her baby when an armed intruder broke in through a first-floor window at the back of the house. It was six o'clock on a spring evening and still daylight.

I had picked up my children from school and was cooking in the kitchen. I had my niece for tea with me and my son at that time was a baby, crawling all over the floor. Emma, my six year old, was upstairs in the bathroom.

All of a sudden out of the corner of my eye, I saw this thing coming down the stairs. At first I thought it was a joke, I thought my husband was playing a trick. Then I realised it was a stranger wearing a balaclava, gloves, and holding a sawn-off shot gun. At first I couldn't accept the reality of it. I was a little surprised.

He said, 'Don't nobody move. This is a robbery.'

I laughed and said, 'Are you kidding, are you joking?'

He was about five foot eight, had short legs and a long body.

His eyes were bluish grey and because his balaclava was torn, I could see a strand of reddish hair. He had very bad teeth.

I could see my niece was terrified, she was standing right next to me, shaking. I didn't feel anything, I wasn't frightened at all. The whole time I was not frightened.

I said to my niece in my language, 'Don't let him know you are afraid. Pick up the baby and hold onto him.'

Then the man said to me, 'I want your jewellery.'

I said, 'Fine, you can have it, I have worn it for many years, it's old now.' I was just making jokes like this. I gave him a Cartier Santos watch and he gave it back to me, so I put it in my pocket and said, 'Thanks very much.' I think that was because I had so many gold bangles, it looked fake. I was wearing earrings and a chain and he didn't notice. He was nervous and shaking. I was quite calm.

He pointed the shot gun at me and at the same time was dropping my things into a bag he had with him. It was quite unreal looking down the two barrels. He said very little. He asked, 'Where's the safe?' I said, 'Would I wear this much jewellery if I had a safe?' He replied, 'We'll check upstairs.'

He motioned with the gun for us to go upstairs. I didn't

think of rape. Rape didn't come into it at all. He asked for jewellery and I thought that's probably what he had come for. As I went up the stairs, all that was in my mind was a vision of my children and myself lying in a pool of blood. This flashed through my mind about five times. And I'm praying, and I'm thinking, Oh God, please, Stephen doesn't deserve this, no not this, he doesn't deserve this. And all the time I was saying 'The Lord is my shepherd.' I'm Catholic and I talk to God all the time.

As I was saying to myself, 'The Lord is my shepherd,' he double backed and locked the front door which set off the alarm. I said to myself, Thank God. God is never asleep.' I said to him, 'Not your day, you haven't planned this very well. The police will be here in three minutes, they usually come very quickly.'

It was a lie because at the time we weren't actually attached to the station. Although we now have a sophisticated system connected direct to the police. I said, 'Just turn the key and it will switch off, but the police will be here in a minute.'

That was when he really panicked. We went upstairs and he followed. As we got into my bedroom my little daughter, hearing voices and thinking Daddy was back, came out of

the bathroom opposite. He grabbed her hair and I grabbed his hand very hard. I thought, You can mess with me, but mess with my kids and you have to shoot me first. I said, 'It's OK, it's only my daughter, she's only six, it's all right, it's only a child.'

I was still squeezing really hard and I felt his hand let go, so I let go. I said, 'Listen, don't be stupid, I'm not going to do anything stupid. Put your gun away, I'm not going to fight you. You can take the house, shrink it, put it in your bag and just blow it up whenever you get to where you're going. Then you can raid it as much as you like, but don't do anything stupid.'

Then he put the gun under his arm. It was still pointing towards me, but his finger wasn't on the trigger. All the time I wanted to keep calm and stop him panicking. Stop him using the gun without meaning to. We all went into the main bedroom and as we entered I saw on the bedside table a thick gold chain which my husband had given to me. I quickly walked to the table and placed a book on the chain.

He said, 'What have you got there?' I picked up some pearls – they were fake pearls which my son loved to play with. He took the pearls and said, 'Oh rubbish.' I said, 'A man of good taste.' He said, 'Do you know what's up here?' I said, 'Well, this is all really. But you've got to get out of here quickly.' He asked, 'Where shall I lock you?' I said, 'Well you can lock us up in this room.' I intended to use the phone in this room. He said, 'No, the front room.'

He seemed to know the house, he must have studied it. I thought maybe he could have been a builder, or a window cleaner, but I didn't recognise him. We went into the front room and he said, 'Don't forget to mention me to the papers, Patti,' and I went, 'Yeah, I sure won't.'

I heard him run down the stairs and throw the key somewhere, I heard it crash into the wall. I heard him smash the back door which was open. All he had to do was turn the handle. He smashed the door open and disappeared around the back.

Meanwhile I was trying to attract the attention of a woman about a hundred feet away down the drive. I was yelling, 'Help, there's a man with a gun in the house,' and I was waving my arms about. The woman was walking past with her daughter and looked up. She came up to the house and I yelled at her to go next-door and call the police. Within five minutes the police were there.

They were wonderful. He must have thought the alarm had got the police because they were there so quickly. One policeman said to me, 'We've just had a call from the *Sun* newspaper saying Patti's been robbed.' It was before mobile phones so the man must have rung from around the corner.

I tried to telephone my husband but when I picked up the phone the line was dead. The police told me that the line had been cut. He had really planned it. He must have known my husband's comings and goings. He must have known the time I was likely to be on my own. Across the road there are a lot of trees and grass. He must have been lying and watching.

My husband came back to find police cars everywhere. He went completely white, but I was calm. I kept thinking to myself, Why aren't you nervous, why aren't you frightened? I couldn't believe we were safe and that the man had actually gone. I kept having flashes of us lying in a pool of blood. But somehow I had remained strong. I always used to remember my mother saying, 'If anyone attacks you, you usually panic if you're on your own, but if you have your children with you, you have the strength of ten thousand lions.' Quite honestly, if he had come with a knife and not a gun he wouldn't have stood a chance. But I know the harm a sawn-off shot gun can do. It could have taken all of us out at the same time and I didn't want to mess with him.

Two months later someone appeared in our garden. Stephen, my husband, had been cleaning the pool and had left the lights on in the garden. I couldn't see his face properly, but I was sure it was the same person. The police said they usually come back.

How were you after the attack?

After the attack I was fine. I didn't think about it, or whenever I did think about it I was amazed at how brave I'd been. And then suddenly about two months later my husband rang a security firm to put bars around the windows and maybe that was what brought it on. I said, 'No, I don't want any bars around the windows. Supposing there's a fire and I'm locked in my house like a caged animal? If he wanted, he could have rung the door bell, I would have opened the door.'

I suddenly went upstairs, sat on the bed and cried. I couldn't get that vision of us all lying in a pool of blood out of my mind, it was so clear. I just couldn't get it out of my mind.

Did you think you could be so calm in such a situation?

Before this happened, you know how you hear on television that someone got robbed and you think, God, if that happened to me, I'd just faint, I'd pass out. He wouldn't have to rob me, I'd be on the floor.

It was nothing like that, I was right on top of everything. It was instinct, I stayed calm. That was the most amazing thing.

6 Trish: Indecent Assault

Trish, a petite housewife in her mid-thirties, experienced indecent assault on a bus early one August morning.

It was a quarter to eight in the morning, I got on the bus and went to the back. There was a rather large gentleman, slouched in his seat, so I sat on the seat facing him. There was a terrible smell coming from this man so I turned away from him. He was in his late forties early fifties, not very tall but very big sideways. He must have weighed well over twenty stone (280 lbs) without exaggeration.

I didn't think that he was a tramp. I found out later that he lived in a hostel for the homeless, that type of thing, so I would imagine he was unemployed but I don't think he would be able to get a job with that odour anyway. There were a good ten persons on the bus downstairs, it was a double decker. There was a young girl on the bus, about twelve years of age, and a few others. When I got to my stop, I stood up to go towards the doors and felt somebody touch me between my legs from behind. I was wearing jeans and a T shirt.

At first I was puzzled because I wondered what it was. I turned around and he was the only person there and I said to him, 'What are you doing?' And

he said, 'You dropped something.' I looked to see what I'd dropped and realised I hadn't dropped anything at all, and I said, 'No, I haven't,' and he said, 'Well, I thought you did.'

Well, I just turned round and very loudly called him a 'dirty, f – bastard.' Everybody heard and everyone looked around but nobody said a word. They just sort of sat there, looking and listening. They didn't say anything.

Meanwhile, he just laid back in the seat, legs akimbo, with a smirk. He wasn't bothered at all by the fact I'd sworn at him. By then I was approaching my bus stop. I felt like slapping him around the face, but I wouldn't have done so. The size of him intimidated me, especially with me being so little, compared to him. I thought I'd just get off the bus and forget about it. But then what crossed my mind was the young schoolgirl on the bus and if it hadn't have been me, then it could have been her. I thought I'd tell the driver what happened so that he could keep an eye on the man.

The driver immediately stopped the bus, made sure all the doors were closed and asked a young woman on the bus if she would go up to the corner where there's usually a policeman on duty. All the time the fat man just sat at the back of the bus smiling to himself.

The woman returned with the policeman who asked me what the problem was. I explained that this man had touched me and the policeman took my name and address, went to the back of the bus and asked the fat man, 'Sir, please can you tell me what's occurred?' The fat man replied, 'Nothing, why, what's bothering you?' And then the policeman said, 'Well, this young lady said you touched her.' And then the policeman said to me, 'Would you like to take this matter further and press charges?' Before I could even answer, the fat man turned round and said, 'If she takes me – if I end up in court – then she'll be dead, I'll make sure that she's dead.' I asked the policeman if he was going to allow this man to say that. The policeman replied to the fat man, 'Now, now, sir, there's no need for that.' I couldn't believe it, I just got off the bus in disgust. I don't know what happened after that. I suppose by my getting off the bus they realised I wasn't going to press charges, and the policeman got off as well.

The driver of the London Transport bus had got the fat man's name and address from the policeman and gave it to me as I was getting off the bus. He was very sympathetic and took it all more seriously. He said that the man had a bus pass and that he would refuse him on his bus in the future. In fact the driver has now been made an Inspector as I have seen him in his Inspector's uniform.

Is there anything you would say to women reading this. What advice would you give them based on your own experience?

I would say don't be embarrassed about making a fuss. Definitely bring it to the attention of other people. I was in two minds about getting off the bus and forgetting about it, but then he could have done something to the next person, especially the young schoolgirl.

Were you annoyed with the policeman?

Yes, I think the policeman should have taken matters into his own hands. Then I would have pressed charges. I was so angry that he let this man threaten me, threaten my life if I were to press charges, that I got off the bus.

Since the incident I have seen my assailant again when I was shopping locally. I got off the bus and he was standing waiting to get on. When I saw him I was angry to start with but then I was scared, intimidated, because I thought if he could do that to me on a bus with people, then I didn't want to meet him in the street alone. You can't believe the size of him.

If it was ever to happen again, I would press charges.

What would you say to women if they are threatened and feel they are not getting enough support from a policeman?

Now I would say, 'Could you please deal with this in the way that the police are meant to. You are supposed to write what he said down, and what he said is a threat and that's got to be against the law.' The threat was more dangerous and upsetting than being touched. These men obviously get their kicks out of doing something like this or they wouldn't do it. Where do they draw the line? Where do they stop?

7 Caron: Attempted Rape

Caron is twenty-two years old and works as civilian staff at Barnet Police Station. Her father has been a policeman there for twenty years. Prior to her working for the police, she was out having a drink with friends when she was attacked on her way to the bus stop.

It was Friday night and I'd been out with my regular group of friends for a drink at my local pub. I left that particular night at half-past ten, which was slightly earlier than usual, to catch the bus home. Instead of walking on the busy side of the street, I cut through an alleyway at the back of the church. It's where wedding photos are taken and has a hedge which is not very high so you can easily see all the grounds. Normally there is a great deal of traffic around, but that night there was absolutely nothing, no-one in sight. So I started running a bit, because I thought I was going to miss the bus.

I remember looking into the grounds beside the pathway and actually thinking, If anyone's going to attack me they're going to come from these grounds, and as they've got a hedge to get over I'm going to hear them, if not see them. I paid absolutely no attention to the wall on my right as there's no way someone can stand there.

I carried on walking. There are two doors set into the wall. I think they both lead to a library. This man must have been standing there and just fell upon me. I thought he was drunk so I pushed him off into the hedge and carried on walking, thinking nothing of it.

I got to the bus stop which is at the end of the alley on the left. I remember looking down the road as I was walking, again amazed that there was no traffic. I looked up the road and waited for the bus to come. No bus, no people, and as I looked back down the road the same man was standing immediately in front of me. I didn't hear him.

I think the first thing I realised was that he was breathing straight into my face. I was shocked and stepped back and he grabbed my belt trying to undo my trousers while his other hand went up my top. I thought he was trying to strip me. I was shocked and couldn't scream, I was frozen. He pushed me on to the hedge and I just kept thinking, What the hell are you doing? God, it's not happening to me, this can't be happening.

He was looking at me and not blinking and he had such strength as he pushed me back into the hedge. I rubbed up against a holly branch and I'd been sunbathing the day before and it brought me to my senses. All of a sudden I realised what was happening to me and got very angry.

I pushed him back and brought my knee up but I don't think it connected with his groin the first time. He fell back into the road quite a long way. He then got up and started coming towards me again and I thought, Oh my God, if something like that's not going to hurt him, what is? I started swearing at him and saying, Piss off, you bastard, what do you think you're doing? Leave me alone. And he kept coming towards me even though I was screaming my lungs out. The only thing I could think of was to do it again, but this time to make sure I hit the right place.

The second kick landed right in his groin. He got up and ran moaning and limping away back down to the High Street. I actually followed him, still shouting abuse at him. I saw two boys sitting in the church yard and I asked them, 'Didn't you hear me shouting, didn't you see him? Couldn't you see what was happening?' They said, 'No, sorry, love.' They were eating a bag of chips and started laughing. I said, 'Well, thanks a lot.'

I was in a bit of a mess, but I managed to pull myself together and run back up to the pub. It was quite embarrassing as there's two entrances to this pub. At the first one I grabbed hold of the door and I was really shaking it and it wouldn't open and I felt a real idiot and had to say to myself, 'Right, compose yourself, this is not the right door.' I then opened the right door and there were a lot of people at the front of the pub and I shouted, 'Move!' And everyone just went, 'Phew,' and parted like the Red Sea. My friend Carolyn came over and she said, 'What's happened? You can tell me.' I broke down into floods of tears. She calmed me down and I told her what had happened. Because my dad's a policeman at High Barnet I didn't want to report it there because I knew too many people and she said she would take me in a car to another station. I thought, Why should I let him get away with it? Why should I sit at home and mull over it? He could go out and do something worse to somebody else. So I reported it.

I reported it from home and two PCs, and a woman WPS turned up. I then went to Whetstone Police Station and stayed there until about half-past four in the morning, giving a statement while it was still fresh in my mind. They did give me a choice, but I preferred to do it then and there. I also drew a picture. I like sketching and I'm good at remembering people's faces.

Two days later, Boris, the man who does the identikit,

sketched my attacker from my description and then we compared my picture with his and there was a definite likeness there. That was good and quite interesting.

How did the incident affect you?

I stayed in for a week doing a jigsaw puzzle which seemed to help me get over it. Then when I was out shopping this bloke came out of one of the shops and literally brushed against me and I turned round and he had the same sort of features and I was thinking, Oh God, is that him? He was a little bit taller, but he was up on a step.

Have you studied martial arts?

Yes, I did Judo for three years, but even so there was no convenient way I could have thrown him. It probably helped me when I kicked him, though.

What did he look like?

He was very dark and dark haired. About five foot eight or nine. I am five foot eleven.

Would you say that women should report an attack?

Definitely. It's embarrassing at the time obviously if you've got to go through it all again, and it might not be particularly pleasant. Even if it was a rape, because a rape could progress to murder, or from an indecent assault it could progress to rape. The list is endless. I mean, you could have been the lucky one out of a lot of people who are not going to be so lucky.

You turned your fear into anger. What do you think would have happened if you had not?

If it had gone the other way, instead of my fear turning into anger, I reckon he would probably have dragged me down the alley and raped me.

It does seem that these type of people are repeat offenders. It isn't that it's going to be some nice man who turns mad for a couple of seconds and then goes on being nice.

Yes, eventually he'll probably think, Well I can get away with that, let's see what else I can get away with.

What would you share about your particular experience with our readers?

Well, if you find a convenient moment for yourself to get away, then by all means just run. But fight back, give yourself a chance to get away.

8 Dragana: Mugging

Dragana is a lively and vivacious mother of two in her mid-thirties. She is a director of a successful advertising agency. One wintry evening she was walking back to her car when she was assaulted.

It was three and a half years ago, when I was at my previous agency which is just off Regents Park in London. I used to park my car in there. I left work one evening in February, at about eight o'clock which was a fairly normal time to leave, and obviously it was dark. I took my usual route to my car, which was in a free car parking area quite close to the zoo, not very far from the office. The route I took was the same as I took every night which was past a pub, past a block of council flats and over a small railway bridge.

I was carrying a briefcase, Marks and Spencers shopping bags and my handbag. Usually there are a few people around at that time of night. Apart from people going in and out of the pub, there's a small tobacconist next door to the pub, so there's people going in and out of that. But once I'd actually crossed that part of the road and was walking towards the bridge there wasn't anybody around.

I suddenly noticed, coming round the corner of the bridge, two young guys. They walked towards me and I did what I suppose one shouldn't do, which is look at them. I thought: This is quite unusual and I should check them out. They were literally parallel with me when I was filled with a sense of foreboding. I just knew I was going to be attacked. I suddenly thought, Ah, it's my turn, and the realisation of that prepared me for what happened next.

As they walked past me, I was sure that they were coming back. I carried on walking up the bridge and then I didn't hear anything, there wasn't any sound at all, and I just turned round and one of them was right in my face. It clearly surprised him that I'd turned round as he had been quite silent, approaching me in his sneakers. Then everything just flashed through my mind. The whole incident must have lasted probably a minute at most, but I remember every single thing that was done and said.

He looked at me and I thought, Well, where's the other one? The other one was actually right on the other side of the street, kind of lurking, looking this way and that. The guy standing in front of me was probably about nineteen, much taller than me. I mean six foot. I'm five foot three. He lurched for my handbag which was of course hanging from my shoulder and it was the arm that I had my briefcase on and I had my shopping in the other hand, so he probably thought, Just give this a yank and it'll be off and I'll be gone. I was thinking, God, he might knife me, or he might knock me to the ground. And because I was standing on the edge of the pavement, I had this ridiculous vision of tomorrow's headlines: Woman dies from blow on head after being thrown to pavement. And I thought that would be a pathetic way to go.

I looked up at him and I remember hearing a squeaky little voice saying, 'No, please don't hurt me.' I thought, This is appalling, how dare he do this! I was filled with rage because I realised that the squeaky little voice was mine and I knew if I just squeaked at him I'd had it. I was filled with absolute rage to think that he could just walk up to me and take whatever he wanted, so I said, 'You've got another think coming!'

I kind of faced up to him as he was pulling at my bag which didn't come off easily because by then I had my briefcase wrapped across me. He was tugging and I was holding on. Then he punched me in the chest to try and make me move back. At that point, I dropped my shopping bag which was in my right hand and hit him really hard thinking, I hope something comes out other than 'Please don't hurt me'.

A little light came on in my head and I remembered all my old drama teachers saying, 'From the diaphragm, darling.' I let out a huge bellow, I mean literally, as if I was being skinned alive. I remember he stepped back and all I could see in his face was, Oh my God, I'm attacking a mad woman. And he ran towards his accomplice. I just stood there. Then I looked up at the flats and there was a woman standing on a fire escape balcony, clearly alerted by my screaming and trying to work out what was happening. I dropped everything and was so outraged that he was running down the street that I started shouting out at him, saying, 'You f – wanker, you can't even attack a woman.' Then I thought, Why are you doing this? He could come back?

I was overwhelmed with fear and sat down on the pavement and burst into tears and this lady came over to me and said, 'Are you all right, what happened?' I could hardly speak, I was crying. She said, 'I haven't got a phone but come with me. Can you stand up? Are you hurt?' I said, 'No, I'm not hurt, I'm fine, I just got winded because he gave me a thump in the chest.'

She took me over to the phone box and said that she would get someone to come out from the pub as well. Within seconds there were all sorts of people outside and then the police turned up in a great white van and scores of them came pouring out. They were charming and extremely helpful. One policeman asked if I would like to phone home. My husband was away on business, my nanny was expecting me home and I was already late, but I just couldn't remember my phone number. He then asked me if I wanted to phone anybody else, but I couldn't remember my mother's or my sister's phone numbers. I couldn't remember anybody's phone number.

So then he said, 'I think you should come down to the station with me and we'll sit you in the canteen and give you a cup of tea and then when you compose yourself a bit we'll see if you can remember where you live.' So they put me in the van and were very friendly and told me that although I had been the first woman who had been jumped on in the street, what had been happening was that gangs of young men had cottoned on to the fact that people from offices around there were parking their cars on this one free bit of parking space in Regents Park and that they'd been going in and doing the cars over. The police had begun to patrol the area and alert the drivers as well. It was clearly opportunistic. I just happened to be walking up the street at that time.

The police recommend that you only fight back if your personal safety is under threat. How do you feel about that?

Mine was an absolutely natural reaction which was just born out of this unbelievable anger, that my space was being invaded in a way that was utterly unacceptable to me. At eight o'clock at night if I can't go home carrying my shopping and my briefcase then what the hell am I supposed to do? I haven't done any self-defence training, but this was just absolute outrage. There was a certainty there that because I'd been prepared, even though it was only for moments, knowing what was happening to me, I thought, Well, you either stand here and take it or you bloody well do something about it. And when I screamed at him so loudly, I reversed the control and suddenly I became much more powerful. I knew he'd go if I kept on screaming.

Going back to what you said earlier, about looking people in the eye, you said you didn't know whether to or not. If you do look them in the eye, you know immediately whether they are a threat or not. If you avert your eyes it shows that you are vulnerable.

I wondered if by making eye contact they would think, Oh,

well, we've sussed her out and she's kind of small. But it enabled me to give the police a very good description. Now, I find myself staring at people and thinking, If he attacks me I'll know exactly what colour eyes he has got. It's quite good training.

Dr Pauline Bart, an expert we consulted, says that pleading, playing the victim's part, is one of the behaviours often associated with rape or assault. But yelling from the diaphragm, which we actually recommend in the book and on the video, gives you a shot of adrenalin.

Yes, it does. I felt that if I had to fight him off, I was in a stronger position to do it and really felt geared up and suddenly alert, whereas before I could only focus on him.

How did you feel after the attack?

I was very nervous for at least a month afterwards. The people in the office were very kind about it. Men were offering either to walk or drive me up to the park. It was quite shortly after that that I got a parking space downstairs. I found that I would drive up and down my street to try and get a spot outside my house, so that I'd walk the shortest distance possible. Now I always get out of the car holding my keys.

Always have my front door key ready. Whereas before I was a classic fumbler, always groping around in the dark, now I'm highly organised.

I think it was brought to a head when one day I was walking, I think probably back from the off licence, not terribly late, and I jumped out of my skin at what turned out to be a hamburger carton that was being blown by the wind behind me. I nearly jumped over a wall I was so frightened and there was nobody there. I remember thinking that I was behaving in a victimised sense which meant that they had won and that's simply not what it's about.

I began to toughen up then, and actually found that things that used to make me slightly embarrassed didn't any more, like if I heard somebody walking behind me I'd turn round and check them out. And if they said anything, I'd just tell them, 'Terribly sorry, but I've been attacked once before and I'm not letting it happen again.' If they looked peculiar in any way I'd cross the road or walk into a shop. I'd be quite happy now going up to somebody's front door and saying, 'Excuse me can I come in for two minutes because I think there's somebody following me?' I know we've been brought up to be nice girls, but it simply wouldn't bother me at all now.

9 Georgina: Attempted Rape

Georgina is thirty-one years old. She was attacked four years ago in her home when she was a mime student. She was staying in a hostel with communal bathrooms and corridors:

I'd been out for the evening and when I got back home round about midnight I noticed that the toilet and the bathroom windows were wide open, and as the flat's on the ground floor, I thought it was a bit strange. Then I saw a guy snooping around outside the flats and thought that he was trying to get in through the bathroom window. I felt really scared and went immediately to a neighbour and got her to call the police. The police turned up about ten minutes later and they had a good look round the flat but there was no sign of this man. I described him as of medium build, with short dark hair, pale skin and blue eyes. We shut all the windows carefully and the police left.

I went into my room and phoned a friend to tell her what had happened and we had a good laugh about it. I then walked out of my room to go to the bathroom and this man was standing there in the hallway in front of me. I said something like, 'What are you doing here?' and he said, 'I'm waiting for

Bill,' and we both knew it was a lie. I stepped back into the bedroom to shut the door. The door had a lock but it was flimsy, not a strong door. My heart was racing and I was thinking about what I should do – should I phone the police again or try getting out of the window? – when he suddenly burst through. He kicked the door in and the lock came flying off.

It is forever engraved in my memory. There was a sort of deliberateness about it that was really scary. He came towards me and I backed into a corner and he said, 'Get your clothes off, get undressed,' and then produced a massive twelve inch screwdriver from his belt which he was holding like a dagger above his head. I had visions of ending up in a pool of blood with multiple stab wounds. I thought that I was going to be attacked. and if I was going to have to fight, I made the decision to fight with my clothes on.

I had this feeling that by keeping my clothes on I would feel stronger, less vulnerable. I felt if I was going to fight, I wouldn't just give in, I would fight to the death. So I refused to get undressed, and I think simply the fact that I refused and stood my ground unnerved him. He was a bit taken aback for a while. He backed off, he didn't come for me like I thought he would. He started saying,

'This isn't really what I came for, it's money I'm after, money I want.' Unfortunately I didn't have any money. I don't know if it would have made any difference if I had, but I said, 'I don't have any.'

I felt that I had some leeway then and tried then to persuade him to go, telling him he was really confused, that he didn't really want to be here and that it would be best if he left now. And I said I wouldn't contact the police. I stayed quite calm in myself, I suppose, and was assessing the situation for it felt like a long period of time. I had an advantage over him in that he'd been drinking and so he wasn't thinking as fast as he could have.

He'd gone into a more composed posture but then he just literally lunged at me and said, 'I want you.' It was a full-blooded charge. I stepped out of the way and he crashed to the ground. I took my chance and ran for it. I ran out of the flat and out into the main hall and up the stairs of the block, screaming my head off. I ran up to the top of the block of flats and started banging on a door. The woman behind the door wouldn't let me in. She just wasn't going to let me in and I was getting more and more desperate, and then someone on the floor below came out, a girl I knew from before and she called me and

said, 'Come here, come here quickly.' And so I went into her flat and we rang the police. They turned up finally but by then he had disappeared.

When I recounted the story later on to a police officer from Scotland Yard his comment on it was that I'd dominated my attacker psychologically. I think there is an element of truth to that but I also think it was stubborn resistance. I think he expected me just to give in and throw all my clothes off and lay myself down for him.

I was very shaken up immediately afterwards and I moved out of the flat the next day. Because it had been a deliberate attack, I was very scared about him coming back so I moved out. I didn't want to go back there for anything. I really was in a state of shock. I think I didn't even recognise myself for a while. I crashed my car the following week and it was only then that I realised how shaken up I was. I had a real fear of being on my own in a house and that fear lasted for a long time. I do routine checking on everything, double checking the windows and the doors, always having an escape plan in the back of my mind should someone come in.

Is there anything you think you've learnt or any advice you could possibly give to other

women faced with the same sort of circumstances?

Yes, I think in my situation, the simple fact of resisting gave me an edge. He wasn't expecting me to be prepared to fight. I'd say to any woman in the same situation, don't give in.

I've thought about it a lot since then and the conclusion I came to was that your own self-esteem is really important, the way that you value yourself. If you value yourself and some-one's trying to attack you, you'll feel really angry about that and that anger is your motivation, is your resistance. So I'd like to say the single most important thing women can do in fact is work on their own self-esteem, loving and valuing themselves, and then they will be clear as to what their boundaries are and what they're really worth.

10 Sarah: Harassment

Sarah is a successful international jewellery designer and manufacturer. After a night out with her flatmate they returned home and were followed by a man.

I was returning home from a nightclub with a girlfriend and as we came through the communal front door of the block, a man walked in behind us. He was tall, well-dressed and looked as though he'd been out to a nightclub. We knew everyone in the flats but didn't recognise this man.

We lived on the seventh floor and as we started to climb the stairs it became pretty obvious that he was loitering behind us. So I said to him, 'Well, what are you doing? Where are you going?' And he said, 'With you.' And I said, 'What do you mean, with us?' And he said, 'Well, I'm coming in with you to have a cup of coffee.'

At that point we were on the third floor and we both said, 'No, you're not.' He said, 'Yes, I'm coming with you.' We told him to leave, but he wouldn't so we had no choice but to get out of the building as we knew as soon as we opened our flat door he would force his way in.

We told him we were going to get the police. We ran down the stairs and across the road into a night club and tried to use the phone. It was a gay club called the Pink Panther. They wouldn't let women in and kicked us out. There wasn't a police car in sight, which is unusual for Soho at that time of the night, so we ran up Oxford Street holding on to each other.

We found a phone box in a passageway just off Oxford Street and we phoned the police. We told them that there was a chap sitting on our staircase and could they come over and sort it out?

By the time we'd walked back to the flat, a police car had arrived. There were three policemen and they let us walk up the stairs first, which I found a little peculiar at the time. We'd been away at least a quarter of an hour, and I thought he would be long gone. Why would he want to stay knowing that we'd gone out to get the police?

When we got to the third floor, there he was sitting on the steps. He didn't even jump up or do anything. The police frisked him and they found a knife in his pocket. He immediately started telling the police that we'd invited him in. He said, 'They invited me in for coffee, what's the big deal?' But the police knew we hadn't or we wouldn't have been so scared. They took him downstairs and put him in the back of the car.

In the meantime, I told one of the policemen what we did

for a living and who we were. I was trying to persuade him that although we lived in Soho, we weren't prostitutes. I thought they might want to come up to the flat and see my jewellery on the tables but they didn't bother, they were only concerned that this man was where he shouldn't be.

They never contacted us again. They never wrote our names down or took any information from us at all. They just took the man away and that was that. I suppose that they could only have charged him with having an offensive weapon. We were both rather scared that one night we might return to see him back on the stairs, but we never did.

What advice would you give to other young women who are followed to their home?

I'd never go into my flat if there was somebody behind me. I might ring someone else's door-bell and go in where there are other people, but I wouldn't go in on my own, that's for sure, or I'd get out of the building and ring the police. I would never confront him.

11 Marian: Attempted Rape

Marian is a lively, attractive woman. Married and a mother of three, she has recently received a BA Hons in sociology. At the time of her attack she was an enrolled nurse and was coming home from a night out with a friend.

This incident took place in the early 1980s, I was thirty years of age.

My friend Laura and I jumped into a local cab which was waiting outside our local disco. We told the driver our destinations and decided it was best to drop me off first and Laura, who lived nearby, last.

When we arrived outside my home I went to pay but Laura said she would pay. I got out and went inside my home.

It was a summer night so I was hot and sticky. I undressed and threw all my clothes into the washing machine and switched it on. As I walked into the hall I picked up the phone to ring a friend to tell him how the night had gone. Then I was going to bed. While I was on the phone there was a knock at the front door. I shouted out, 'Who is it?' and told Jeff, my friend, to hang on the line a minute. The reply through the door was something like, 'It's the taxi driver, I've found your purse on the back seat of my taxi.' I told him to push it through the letter box.

He whined that it wouldn't go through the letter box. I told Jeff I would phone him back and rung off.

At the front door I peered through the small window and shouted to the taxi driver, 'It's OK, put it through the letter box.' Again he whined, 'I can't, it won't go through,' so I thought, Oh for goodness sake, and I opened the door just enough to allow him to hand me my purse. I also positioned my leg by the door to prevent it from opening too far. I wasn't wearing any clothes and didn't want him to see.

The taxi driver handed over my purse and said, 'Just check your money is still there.' I wanted to get rid of him so I let go of the catch to check my money and he forced the door open. The force caused me to jump backwards. I was startled and frightened and he began to walk towards me and I stepped back. He was trembling and said, 'Oh duck, I don't half fancy you, can I come in?' He was already in the hall, walking towards me. Everything happened so quickly.

I felt weak, sick, and a part of me was saying, This isn't real, this isn't really happening. Time seemed to stand still. His hands came towards my shoulders and I remember thinking, Oh God, he's going to rape me. Suddenly, just before his hands touched my shoulders, I pushed him with all my strength. He grabbed hold of the sitting-room doorway and with the other hand he grabbed hold of the staircase. I pushed him again and this time he fell back, grabbing hold of the front door frame.

At this point I really thought I had no strength left and I got very, very angry. I drew my right knee up into his groin and dug my long nails into his throat. I screamed, 'Get out of my house you dirty pig!' and pushed him really hard. I then slammed the front door and shook with relief. I still couldn't believe what had happened. I remember thinking what an idiot I was to open the door. I kept repeating, 'You dirty pig, dirty pig.' I couldn't believe it. I was talking to myself and really shaking, I felt contaminated. I rubbed my arms where his jacket had touched me. Then I rang Jeff back.

He calmed me down, asked me questions like, did he hurt me, could I describe him, what taxi was he driving, did I want to report him?

Eventually I calmed down enough to ring off. I made a cup of coffee and went to bed. I blamed myself for everything. I thought the police would only blame me. I didn't report it.

The next morning I had an anonymous phone call. It was a man's voice asking me if I was all right. I asked who is it, but they repeated, 'Are you all right?' I replied something like, 'It depends what you call all right, I suppose I am.' They hung up and to this day I don't know who made that call. I did not recognise the voice.

I felt stupid. I told all my friends about the incident. We all agreed we should take greater care of each other, such as one of us would remain sober and look after the rest of us on a night out. We were all wary of taxi drivers. I myself would walk home rather than get in a taxi. This lasted for about six months. I felt guilty for not reporting the incident; he must have tried this on other women.

What advice would you give other women reading this book?

From my experience of this attack I would advise others to listen to that voice inside, believe in your feelings and what your senses are telling you. I acted, I fought back. I was lucky too. I think because he didn't expect me to fight back and I took advantage of that and didn't hesitate. What have you got to lose?

12 Dinah: Violent Rape

Dinah is an attractive woman with piercing blue eyes. She is now in her late-forties. Thirty years ago, when she was an eighteen-year-old student, she was violently attacked and raped. She managed to disable her rapist and get away. She has since become a rape crisis counsellor and university lecturer.

It was in 1962 when I was an undergraduate at Nottingham University. I was about eighteen years old and had come up to Nottingham from the country and was therefore pretty unprepared either by my family or indeed by the university for life in the 'Big City'.

It was my first term and one Saturday morning I met a group of friends on Slab Square in the centre of Nottingham. One of the group was a man whom I assumed to be a friend of one of my friends. This man said he was a hairdresser and offered to cut my hair. He was slightly over six foot, fairly well built, strong and probably in his-late twenties. I can't remember anything about his face. I've completely blanked out his face.

I went with him to his flat and he cooked me lunch. I didn't feel threatened at all. Somehow or other it seemed to me that it was OK because it was daytime. I remember think-ing because it was lunch that it was safe, which looking back was naive and foolish. I think if he'd invited me to come back in the evening I would have had second thoughts about it; I certainly would have checked out to see whether anybody knew him or not. I think people still make assumptions like this. You are much more likely to go on an impulse date at lunchtime than if they invite you out in the evening.

Do you think women believe that there are stereotypical times and stereotypical men when it comes to rape?

Yes, I do. After lunch, I sat at his dressing table with a mirror and he cut my hair. Then, all of a sudden, he came up behind me, picked me up bodily and literally threw me on the bed. I think he said something that indicated that because I'd come to his house he assumed that I was willing to have sex with him. He thought it was automatic. You know, the next natural thing to do after feeding someone and giving them a haircut was to pick them up, throw them on the bed and ravish them.

At first I argued and reasoned but he hit me hard over the head with an open hand. It was very painful and very, very frightening. I verbally remonstrated and fought hard.

Up until then I'd always thought that if a woman didn't want to be raped then she didn't have to be. I thought it was difficult for someone to hold open your legs and hold both your arms down all at the same time.

I was quite a wiry little thing. I was twisting and turning, pushing and pummelling. But if you get beaten into submission then eventually you more or less do what you're told to do.

He frightened me when he hit me and it was quite clear to me that there would be more of the same. I quietened down a bit. I was wearing Dr Scholl sandals and remember taking the sandals off and trying to break the window at the top of the bed. I thought if I could break the window, I could attract somebody's attention. But it was very thick glass and I didn't get very far with that.

I think this made him quite angry, looking back. He beat me hard around the head repeatedly and terrorised me into submission, enough to force me to take my clothes off. I thought trying to break the window would bring about a halt to the proceedings. Also, symbolically, doing something like that was a move to convince myself that this was serious. It was a gradual psychological recognition, in fairly slow stages, that I was in a dangerous and horrific situation.

My first instinct was to deny it. You think, This isn't happening to me! This is something else. He's just trying it on, he'll come round. But it became clear to me that he was determined to have sexual intercourse.

In 1962 there was no AIDS but what worried me most beyond getting killed was getting pregnant. I tried to persuade him to use a condom. I thought my best course of action was to go along with it, accommodate him, providing nothing happened which would have disastrous consequences. I was worried about venereal disease and pregnancy and at that time it was very difficult to get an abortion. I didn't want the trauma of that.

That morning I had bought some condoms to use with my boyfriend who was also at the university and I decided to make a deal with my attacker, saying something like, 'OK, you win, I'll have sex with you, but you must use a condom.'

He agreed to use the condom. I was so intimidated that I undressed, taking my jeans and underwear off. He then proceeded to have intercourse with me, using a condom. At that point he wasn't violent, he was just having ordinary sex. Suddenly he stopped, tore off the condom and said he couldn't feel anything. He pulled the condom off and threw it aside and at that point I realised I was in a very serious situation which could have extremely damaging consequences. I also began to think he was mad and that if I wasn't careful and didn't do the right things, he might kill me. I felt very isolated, very cut off from any source of help. I realised that I had to rely on my own resources. I had gone along with it thinking I could use my will, but suddenly I had to use my wits in order to survive. It felt like a gear change.

Up until then I was too frightened, had not got angry enough to do him real physical damage. Then I remembered something that my father had told me, which was if I ever got into that situation to go for a man's testicles because they were the most vulnerable part. So I actually allowed him to enter me again, put my hand down, got hold of his testicles, squeezed as hard as I could and wrenched him round, digging my nails in hard enough to draw blood. He shouted and grabbed hold of himself. He was literally paralysed. I jumped off the bed and started putting my jeans back on. I was getting frustrated because in the sixties jeans were skin tight and it took me much longer getting dressed than if they'd had wider legs.

I got dressed and grabbed my things, unlocked the door and had my hand on the handle when he recovered enough to hit me so hard that I went right across the room and ended up under the table. But despite this attack, I had hurt him enough to make him lose interest in doing anything else except get rid of me. The last thing on his mind was sex. He was also very, very angry with me saying, 'Look what you've done to me,' as though I were the aggressor and he was the victim.

I did not go to the police and I did not go for counselling because at that time there was no where to go. I thought everyone's assumption would be that it was my fault for having gone to his flat in the first place. The only person I told was my boyfriend who punished me further by accusing me of fabricating the whole story in order to cover up an affair. That betrayal was very damaging to me on top of my attack.

After that, I kept completely quiet about my ordeal. I didn't tell my parents, I don't even think I told my sister to whom I was quite close.

I felt stupid, I felt it was my fault. I thought that people would find it a repellent experience and that part of that repellence would be for my role in it. I felt tainted, polluted – but there was another part of me that was very proud of myself. I felt that once I had recognised my position, I had taken swift and strong action. I remember when I grabbed his balls and squeezed them that I could not be half-hearted about it. I really went over the top and that gave me a tremendous sense of confidence in my ability to think my way out of a situation and to act decisively. That belief has stayed with me all my life.

It was probably eighteen months before I could share it at all. I can't remember who I told, it would have been a friend, nobody professional. I wasn't really able to start sharing it until I used it as a way of helping others, which I eventually did by working as a rape crisis counsellor at the Polytechnic in Liverpool, ten years later. I was with a group of women and somebody said the Rape Crisis Centre needed volunteers.

It made me feel as though my experience had not been in vain, that I could use it to empower other people.

What would you recommend to women who have been through an experience of rape, even if they could not escape?

I would absolutely recommend anyone to work through the emotional after-effects of such an assault by taking counselling. It makes you realise that this is something that happens to other people, that it wasn't abnormal or unusual to be abused in this way. Being a woman is partly to do with avoiding these sorts of experiences, and the fact that life can still have them in store for you. Because I didn't deal with it afterwards, the rape had knock-on consequences. I felt that I was implicated – I had made a deal, I had negotiated, colluded – and that did me quite a lot of psychological damage. I was also suspicious of men which changed the nature of my future relationships.

Also, if you possibly can, fight back. Partly because it can save your life and it can get you out of that situation. And partly because the experience is less damaging if you fight back. I turned around and attacked my attacker and *won*. I felt a tremendous sense of pride and power at that which has lasted me right through my life and I think will continue to serve me.

You found out that your attacker had a record?

It turned out that he was an out-patient of a mental hospital in Nottingham and had a history of raping women in order to father children. That certainly fitted in with my intuition about the person I had been locked in the room with, that he was mad. But I think it would help women to recognise that any man who resorts to rape is mad – severely distorted and severely disabled as a person. It is not that the woman is in a room with a normal person who has somehow had this behaviour triggered off by something she may have done. It is his fault, not hers.

Many years later you studied a martial art called Tai–Chi. Tell us about that.

I think that perhaps one of the most useful activities that I've done in terms of regaining and retaining a sense of balance and control over my body is learning Tai–Chi, which teaches you that there is some element of attack in retreat. It teaches you not to polarise by going entirely into an attack or entirely into a retreat and defence, but to retain some element of both.

In terms of women's self-defence training, I think that's a very important lesson for anyone to learn.

In the event of an attack we would urge you to report it to the police. Nowadays, they are most sympathetic and will treat your predicament with consideration and seriousness.

We also recommend that you take counselling. According to the hundreds of women we have heard from, it is proven to be extremely beneficial in aiding recovery from such trauma.

Although not all the centres listed here are called 'Rape Crisis', they should all deal with the area of support. Most of the services operate an answerphone at times when they are not open. These times will vary according to the extent of the services they provide.

Where two telephone numbers are supplied, the first is a counselling helpline and the second is the office number.

Aberdeen
PO Box 123,
Aberdeen

Aberystwyth
c/o Val, 24 Heol–y–Bannau,
Pontrhyfendigaid,
Ystrad Meurig,
Dyfed SY25 6AZ
☎ 0974 5656

Andover
Churchill Bungalow,
Admiral's Way,
Andover
☎ 0264 336 222

Antrim
☎ 084 94 65 256

Avon
PO Box 665,
Bristol, BS99 1XY
☎ 0272 351 707

Aylesbury
☎ 0296 392 468

Ayr
PO Box 45,
Ayr,
Scotland, KA8 8BT
☎ 0292 611 301
☎ 0292 611 298

Ayrshire
PO Box 23,
Kilmarnock, KA1 1DP
☎ 0563 41769
☎ 0563 44686

Bangor
The Abbey Road Centre,
9 Abbey Road,
Bangor,
Gwynedd, LL57 2EA
☎ 0248 354 885

Barnsley
PO Box 72,
Barnsley
☎ 0226 298 560

Basingstoke
Chute House,
Lower Church Street,
Basingstoke, RG21 1QT
☎ 0256 840 224
☎ 0256 843 810

Belfast
41 Waring Street,
Belfast
☎ 0232 249 696
☎ 0232 321 830

Birmingham
PO Box 558,
Deritend
Birmingham, B12 0LS
☎ 021 766 5366
☎ 021 766 5539

Borders
PO Box 7
Galashields, TD1 1SX
☎ 0896 501 00

Bradford
31 Manor Row,
Bradford,
W Yorkshire, BD1 4PS
☎ 0274 308 270
☎ 0274 723 896

Brighton
PO Box 232,
Brighton
E Sussex, BN2 2TY
☎ 0273 203 773

Burton on Trent
c/o Pam Stewart,
93 Nelson Street,
Winshill,
Burton on Trent, DE15 0DE

Cambridge
Box R,
12 Mill Road,
Cambridge
☎ 0223 358 314

Canterbury
The Mustard Seed,
9 St Johns Place, Northgate,
Canterbury, CT1 1BD
☎ 0227 450 400

Cardiff
PO Box 338,
Cardiff,
S Wales, CF1 3TY
☎ 0222 373 181

Central Scotland
PO Box 48,
Stirling
☎ 0786 717 71

Chelmsford
PO Box 566,
Chelmsford, CM2 8YP
☎ 0245 492 123

Chester & Ellesmere Port
PO Box 280,
St John Street, Chester
☎ 0244 317 922

Chesterfield
SAIL,
PO Box 8,
Chesterfield, S40 1NY
☎ 0246 556 114

Cleveland
PO Box 31,
Middlesborough
☎ 0642 225 787
☎ 0642 223 885

Clonmel
14 Wellington Street,
Clonmel, Co Tipperary
☎ 010 353 52 24111

Colchester
    PO Box 548,
    Colchester,
    Essex
    ☎ 0206 769795

Cork
    Box 42,
    Brain Born Street,
    Cork
    ☎ 021 968 086

Cornwall
    PO Box 18,
    Camborne, TR14 8XQ
    ☎ 0209 713 407

Coventry
    c/o CVSC,
    PO Box 8,
    58–64 Corporation Street,
    Coventry, CV1 1GF
    ☎ 0203 677 229
    ☎ 0203 713 372

Croydon
    PO Box 908,
    London, SE25 5EL
    ☎ 081 688 0332
    ☎ 081 688 0334

Carlisle & Cumbria
    PO Box 34,
    Carlisle
    Cumbria, CA1 1EZ
    ☎ 0228 365 00

Derby
    PO Box 142,
    Victoria Street
    Derby, DE1 2YG
    ☎ 0332 372 545

Derry
    PO Box 32,
    Derry, BT48 6BW
    ☎ 0504 260 566

Doncaster
    PO Box 11,
    Doncaster,
    S Yorkshire, DN2 5DR
    ☎ 0302 360 421
    ☎ 0302 341 572

Dublin
    70 Lower Leeson Street,
    Dublin 2
    ☎ 010 353 161 4911
    Fax: 610 873

Dundee
    PO Box 83,
    Dundee
    ☎ 0382 201 291

Durham County
    PO Box 106,
    Darlington, DL3 7YS
    ☎ 0325 369 933
    ☎ 0325 362 996

East Dorset
    PO Box 877,
    Poole,
    Dorset, BH14 8YL
    ☎ 0202 433 950

Edinburgh
    PO Box 120,
    Brunswick Road
    Edinburgh,
    EH7 5XX
    ☎ 031 556 9437
    ☎ 031 557 6737

Enniskilen
☎ 0232 322 210

Exeter
PO Box 123,
Exeter, EX4 3RR
☎ 0392 430 871

Fife
PO Box 4,
Kirkcaldy,
Fife
☎ 0592 642 232

Galway
15a Mary Street,
Galway
☎ 091 64983

Gloucestershire
PO Box 16,
Gloucester, GL4 0RU
☎ 0452 526 770

Halton
PO Box 13,
Widnes,
Cheshire, WA8 7UJ
☎ 051 423 4192
☎ 051 423 4251

Herts Area
PO Box 21,
Ware
☎ 070 72 76512

Highlands
PO Box 10,
Dingwall,
Rosshire,
Scotland, IV15 9LH
☎ 0349 653 16

Hull
PO Box 40, Hull
☎ 0482 299 90

Kendall
Postal Buildings,
Ash Street,
Windemere, LA23 3EB
☎ 0539 734 743

Kirlees
c/o National Childrens
Centre,
New North Parade,
Huddersfield, HD1 5JP
☎ 0484 450 040

Lancaster
PO Box 2, Lancaster
☎ 0524 382 595

Leeds
PO Box 27,
Wellington Street,
Leeds, LS2 7EG
☎ 0532 440 058
☎ 0532 441 323

Leicester
70 High Street,
Leicester, LE1 5YP
☎ 0533 706 990
☎ 0533 702 977

Letterkenny
☎ 074 23 067

Limerick
PO Box 128,
Limerick House,
Limerick
☎ 061 412 11

Littlehampton
PO Box 623,
Littlehampton
W Sussex, BN17 7QZ
☎ 0903 726 411

Liverpool
PO Box 64,
Liverpool, L69 8AP
☎ 051 727 7599
☎ 051 727 7603

London
PO Box 69,
London, WC1X 9NJ
☎ 071 837 1600
☎ 071 278 3956

Luton
12 Oxford Road,
Luton
☎ 0582 334 26
☎ 0582 335 92

Manchester
PO Box 366,
Manchester, M60 2BS
☎ 061 834 8784
☎ 061 839 8379

Medway
69 Woodstock Road,
Stroud,
Rochester Kent, ME4 2DJ
☎ 0634 811 703

Merthyr Tydfil
c/o Merthyr MIND,
11 Glebeland Street,
Merthyr Tydfil,
Mid Glamorgan, CF47 8AD
☎ 0685 721 927

Mid Mersey
PO Box 119,
Liverpool Road,
St Helens
☎ 0744 454 064
☎ 0744 454 063

Milton Keynes
c/o David Baxter Centre,
63 North Seventh Street,
Central Milton Keynes,
Bucks, MK9 2DP
☎ 0908 691 969
☎ 0908 670 312

Newark
ISAS, 85 Millgate,
Newark,
Nottinghamshire
☎ 0636 610 313

Northampton
PO Box 206,
Northampton, NN1 1NF
☎ 0604 250 721

Norwich
PO Box 47, Norwich,
Norfolk, NR1 2BU
☎ 0603 667 687

North Staffs
PO Box 254,
Hanley,
Stoke on Trent, ST1 4RE
☎ 0782 204 177

Nottingham
37a Mansfield Road,
Nottingham
☎ 0602 410 440
☎ 0602 470 064

Oxford
PO Box 20,
Oxford, OX3
☎ 0865 726 295

Peterborough
c/o The Woman's Centre,
18 Crawthorne Road,
Peterborough, PE1 4AB
☎ 0733 340 515

Plymouth
Box A,
Virginia House,
Palace Street,
Plymouth, PL4 0FQ
☎ 0752 223 584
☎ 0752 263 600

Portsmouth
PO Box 3,
Portsmouth, Hampshire
☎ 0705 669 511
☎ 0705 669 513/4

Reading
PO Box 397, Reading
Berks, RG1 5JZ
☎ 0734 575 577
☎ 0734 311 940

Rugby
ROSA, c/o Julia Smith,
40 King Edward Road,
Rugby, CV21 2TA

Sandwell
PO Box 2223,
Oldbury, Warley,
W Midlands, B69 4HJ
☎ 021 552 9811
☎ 021 552 9799

Scunthorpe
PO Box 76,
Scunthorpe,
S Humberside
☎ 0724 853 953

Sheffield
PO Box 34,
Sheffield, S1 1UD
☎ 0742 755 255
☎ 0742 757 130

Shropshire
PO Box 89,
Wellington,
Telford, TF1 1TZ
☎ 0952 504 666

Southend
54 Queens Road,
Southend
☎ 0702 347 933

Southampton
PO Box 50,
Head Post Office,
Southampton
☎ 0703 701 213

South Essex
Bridgehouse,
160 Bridge Road, Grays
Essex, RM17 6DB
☎ 0375 380 609
☎ 0375 381 322

South West Herts
c/o CVS,
St Thomas Centre,
Langley Road,
Watford, Herts
☎ 0923 241 600

Strathclyde
 PO Box 53,
 Glasgow, G2 1YR
 ☎ 041 221 8448
 ☎ 041 248 2579

Suffolk
 PO Box 135,
 Ipswich, IP1 2QQ
 ☎ 0473 715 333

Swansea
 ☎ 0792 648 805

Swindon
 PO Box 57,
 Swindon, SN5 8AZ
 ☎ 0793 616 511

Tamworth
 SAVAS,
 c/o Cherry Orchard
 Day Hospital,
 Hospital Street,
 The Leys, Tamworth

Tyneside
 34 Grainger Street,
 Newcastle
 ☎ 091 232 9858
 ☎ 091 222 0272

Waterford
 PO Box 57,
 Waterford
 ☎ 010 353 517 3362

Wirral
 PO Box 20, Wallasey,
 Merseyside, L44 9HE
 ☎ 051 666 1392
 ☎ 051 653 5121

Worcester
 PO Box 60,
 Worcester, WR1
 ☎ 0905 724 514

York
 c/o 11 Holgate Road,
 Women's Centre,
 York
 ☎ 0904 610 917

DEFENCE AND MARTIAL ARTS TRAINING

Contact your local police for self-defence classes.

For information on martial arts telephone 0891 11 1314

Please note that where self defence classes are advertised, check that there are trained instructors. Contact either your local police or the Sports Council for further advice.

Martial Arts Governing Bodies

British Aikido Board
Mrs S Timms
☎ 0753 819086

N. Ireland Aikido Association
Mr C Simms
☎ 0232 424336

British Council of Chinese
Martial Arts
Mr C Ellerker
☎ 0732 848065

British Karate Federation
Mrs B Mumberson
☎ 0834 813774

English Karate Governing Body
Mr M Dinsdale
☎ 081 504 6162

N. Ireland Karate Board
Mr M Leyden
☎ 0232 613706

Scottish Karate Board
Mr A Murdoch
☎ 0698 357322

Welsh Karate Federation
Mrs B Mumberson
☎ 0834 813774

British Kendo Association
Mr C Wheaton
☎ 071 608 3502

N. Ireland Kung Fu Association
Mr P Gilligan
☎ 0232 663935

British Ju Jitsu Association
Mr J Steadman
☎ 051 722 6751

N. Ireland Ju Jitsu Association
Mr D Toney
☎ 0232 691811

N. Ireland Martial Arts
Commission
Mr K McLean
☎ 0232 381222 Ext 250

British Taekwondo Council
Mr R M K Choy
☎ 081 429 0878

Taekwondo Association of
Northern Ireland
Mr B Nicholson
☎ 0232 611599

U.K. Tang Soo Do Federation
Mr M K Loke
☎ 0375 386225

ACKNOWLEDGMENTS

Automobile Association of Great Britain

Bart, Pauline, Dr
Sociologist, University of Illinois, USA. Author of *Stopping Rape. Successful Survival Strategies*, Pergamon Press, 1985

Broadcasting Standards Council Survey 1990, 'Women Viewing Violence'

Fein, Judith, PHD
PHD in exercise, psychology, physical education and personal defence programmes, and author of *Are You A Target"* Torrance Publishing Company, 1981/8

FBI, US Justice Department *Crime Tables 26 and 27*, 1985

Home Office Study No. 106, HMSO publications, 1989

Kelly, Liz, Dr
Senior Research Officer, Child Abuse Studies Unit, University of North London

Kennedy, Helena, QC
Barrister and author of *Eve was Framed,* Chatto and Windus Ltd, 1992

Metropolitan Police Public Carriage Office, Islington, London

O'Neil, Jean
National Crime Prevention Commission of America

Steadman, John
6th Dan Ju–jitsu, 1st Dan Karate. National coach and examiner. Self-defence expert

Stockdale, Jan, Dr
Senior Lecturer in Social Psychology, London School of Economics

Stokes, Trish
Rape and Sexual Abuse Support Centre

Strong, Sanford
International crime defence instructor and author (forthcoming publication *Strong On Defence*). Ex San Diego police officer

Temkin, Jennifer, Professor
Professor of Law, Sussex University. Author of *Rape and the Legal Process,* Sweet and Maxwell, 1987